Gaishi

GAISHI
The Foreign Company in Japan

T.W. KANG

BasicBooks
A Division of HarperCollins*Publishers*

Library of Congress Cataloging-in-Publication Data
Kang, T.W.
   Gaishi : the foreign company in Japan / T.W. Kang.
     p.   cm.
   Includes bibliographical references and index.
   ISBN 0-465-02660-5 : $22.95
   1. Corporations, Foreign—Japan. 2. New business
enterprises—Japan. I. Title.
HD2907.K295   1990   90-80251
338.8'8852—dc20   CIP

To my parents,
Ha Koo Kang and Sung In Kim,
who had the foresight to give me
an international education,
and to my patient wife, Yong Jean Park.

Contents

Preface

AS RECENTLY AS THE EARLY 1960s, no one in the world would have been able to imagine the Japan of today. During the time I was growing up there, almost anything from the United States was a curiosity. Those who could afford it spoke proudly of owning a *gaisha* ("foreign car") or a General Electric refrigerator. I had a relative who was stationed at a U.S. Army base in Japan, and anything he brought from the post exchange immediately became a popular item among the neighborhood children. An especially big hit was the original version of the G.I. Joe doll.

Back then, the Japanese looked at Americans with awe. The long isolationism prior to the 1868 Meiji Restoration and the two world wars had left Japan technologically impoverished. Japanese students were taught—and still are—that Japan has no natural resources, and that if human resources are not fully utilized the island will sink. The Japanese were willing to barter any personal capabilities they had for American know-how. Unbelievable as it may seem, Japanese working in *gaishi*s ("foreign-affiliated firms") actually considered themselves to be lucky.

Things are different today. American cars have practically disappeared from Japanese streets, and American consumer appliances are all but unknown in Japanese kitchens. Toys found in American stores are often made either in Japan or somewhere else in the Orient.

Today Japanese industry is a gold mine of know-how, with many firms becoming net exporters of technology. Japanese who work at *gaishi*s are increasingly being perceived as mavericks and cultural deviants. Japan is no longer a source of inexpensive labor; the Japanese today are subcontracting for cheaper labor not only in the newly industrializing economies such as Korea, Taiwan, Hong Kong, and Singapore but also in developing countries. As a nation Japan is quite rich, and its trading partners have been viewing Japan's trade surplus as a threat to world economic stability.

This dramatic evolution took place in a very short period of time, and businesspeople on both sides of the Pacific have still not fully adjusted to it. As late as 1973, I crossed the Pacific and attended Massachusetts Institute of Technology and Harvard Business School in order to get the best possible education in technology and management. Within a decade of my arrival in the United States, Japan had come to dominate such product segments as low-priced automobiles, consumer electronics, and dynamic memory semiconductors; and I began to wonder why I had ever left the country that now seemed to have the most to teach about areas that interested me. Many Japanese executives cannot relinquish their long-held belief that Japan is still a poor country, a perception no doubt encouraged by the Japanese emphasis on institutional over individual wealth. Meanwhile American executives have not entirely faced the fact that those poor and desperate Japanese, who were subservient to the Americans, are influencing American business.

The problem is exacerbated by the cultural distance between the United States and Japan. Unlike the United States, which has a history of a little more than three and a half centuries, Japan is a nation whose cultural values have solidified over two thousand years. The United States is a nation founded on the principle of *e pluribus unum*. Japan is an island nation that has never suffered a major military or business infiltration in its recorded history. This means that where many American business practices can be discussed explicitly, Japanese business practices are founded in folklore and largely tacit. Let me quote from a book written in 1906 by Lafcadio Hearn, one of the earliest Japanophiles:

A thousand books have been written about Japan; but among these,—setting aside artistic publications and works of a purely special character,—the really precious volumes will be found to number scarcely a score. This fact is due to the immense difficulty of perceiving and comprehending what underlies the surface of Japanese life. (P. 3)

I should not be surprised to see a book about Japan written by a contemporary Western writer that started out similarly.

This book examines both of these topics—increasing Japanese influence in global industries and cultural distance between the United States and Japan—particularly as they relate to the American firm trying to penetrate the Japanese market. I write as a global businessperson with management experience on both sides of the Pacific; I have sold, negotiated, hired, trained, and motivated both in the United States and Japan. Moreover, I am in a unique position to discuss the differences in U.S. and Japanese business practices because I am a citizen of neither country. Although I feel strongly about some of the issues covered in this book, my advocacy is not compelled by simple loyalty to either nation. As a Korean fluent in both Japanese and English I have made cultural adjustments in both directions—in 1973 when I moved from Japan to the United States, and in 1985 when I returned to Japan. These adjustments were not easy, and they required that I think intensively about what distinguishes the two countries.

As with any endeavor of this sort, I received much support from various individuals. Although it is impossible to thank all those who helped me in subtle but significant ways, I should like to express my appreciation to Professors Robert H. Hayes and Dennis Encarnation of the Harvard Business School; my friend Ravi Agarwal, for reading through the manuscript; Martin Kessler, Jennifer Fleissner, and Phoebe Hoss of Basic Books for their persistent support; and Robert Markel, who offered his generous help all along the way; my friends at Intel; and my family, who showed much patience during the writing of this book.

Introduction

AMERICAN BUSINESSES CANNOT BE faulted for their lack of adventurousness when it comes to participating in foreign markets. Today one sees Americans doing business in such distant places as Southeast Asia, India, Africa, and the Middle East. Indeed, in many respects, American business is exemplary in its willingness to deal with different cultures.

Japan is the exception. Americans have proved extremely conservative, even defensive, in their efforts to penetrate the Japanese market. A number of years ago, the consulting firm Booz, Allen, and Hamilton studied direct foreign investment in Japan and found that Americans were passive about investing in the Japanese market for two reasons: the sheer complexity of doing business in Japan and the lower short-term profitability of the Japanese market when measured against average corporate profitability expectations.

A vicious cycle is operating here. The Japanese business environment *is* difficult to break into, so American businesses take a conservative attitude. The result is a worsening of the U.S. trade deficit, which leads the U.S. government to pressure Japan to "level the playing field." Often American businesses then relax their competitive efforts against the Japanese, particularly in the Japanese market, on the assumption that "the Japanese are unfair anyway, so no matter what we do, they aren't going to buy from us."

This vicious cycle is extremely dangerous, since in industries where the Japanese tend to become influential, competing in the Japanese market and competing globally against the Japanese are two sides of the same coin. I know because I have done both—sold into the Japanese market and competed against the Japanese in the United States.

Japanese who enter the American market often alter the basis of competition by raising the American customer's expectations about quality, cost, delivery, and service, which collectively are referred to as *QCDS* throughout this book. When the gap between QCDS levels of a Japanese firm and those of its American counterpart are large, the Japanese competitor quickly sets up distribution channels and takes away market share while the American firm scrambles to improve its QCDS ability. Those high customer expectations often existed in the Japanese market years before the Japanese firm entered the American market. If the American firm had competed against the Japanese in the Japanese market and adapted its global ability to those levels, the Japanese firm would have had a much harder time entering the U.S. market. Moreover, when Japanese competitors dominate in the Japanese market, they accumulate the cash resources to plan an offensive. If an American firm succeeds in taking a sizable share of the Japanese market, the war chest of resources required by the Japanese competition to pull off successful entry into the U.S. market is usually reduced.

Finally, in industries in which the Japanese domestic market constitutes a large portion of the world market, taking all of the domestic market gives the Japanese a considerable cost advantage by permitting economies of scale. Thus, in such situations, forfeiting the Japanese market often places the American firm at an operational disadvantage even in non-Japanese markets.

This book, then, is about global competitiveness from the standpoint of the American firm in the Japanese market. There are many books by academics, consultants, and senior executives about industry competitiveness from the perspective of public policy and corporate strategy. But such books do not motivate organizations or individuals to take action. People in U.S. firms still tend to seek refuge in the actions of government and top management. This book deals with "street level" aspects of selling, hiring, training, and partnering—that is, the areas in which the uncertainties of dealing in a widely different culture make American firms skeptical about trying to penetrate the Japanese market, however strong their conviction that doing so is the key to global competitiveness.

THE CULTURAL GAP

The relationship between the United States and Japan continues to challenge and at times frustrate, whether one looks at the relationship between the two governments or at that between Japanese and American firms. Consider, for example, the famous "side letter" to the 1986 Japan-U.S. semiconductor trade agreement. During the last days of negotiations, the U.S. government asked the Japanese government to guarantee American semiconductor manufacturers a target market share of 20 percent in Japan. Because the Japanese government apparently could not do so in public, a side letter was drafted to satisfy this American need. I cite parts of the text of this side letter (now in the public domain), and ask a few questions pertinent to American businesspeople who desire to do business in Japan, to illustrate how different interpretations can be, even when the English language is the common medium.

Both governments are desirous of enhancing free trade in semiconductors on the basis of market principles and the competitive positions of their respective industries. The government of Japan welcomes a significant increase in imports and sales of foreign-based semiconductors in the Japanese market through free and fair competition.

Does the expression "free trade" mean the same thing in the Japanese and American contexts? What does "market principles" mean? How about "free and fair competition"?

The government of Japan recognizes the U.S. semiconductor industry's expectation that semiconductor sales in Japan of foreign capital–affiliated companies will grow to at least slightly above 20 percent of the Japanese market in five years. . . . The attainment of such an expectation depends on competitive factors, the sales efforts of the foreign-affiliated companies, the purchasing efforts of the semiconductor users in Japan and the efforts of both governments.

How good do "the sales efforts of the foreign-affiliated companies" have to be? What does the phrase "purchasing efforts of the semiconductor users in Japan" mean? Are they really going to help out?

The government of Japan will encourage Japanese users to purchase more foreign-based semiconductors and to provide further support for expanded sales by foreign capital–affiliated semiconductor companies in Japan through the establishment of an organization to provide sales assistance for foreign capital–affiliated semiconductor companies and through promotion of long-term relationships between Japanese semiconductor purchasers and foreign capital–affiliated semiconductor companies. . . . The objective of the Arrangement is for long-term, stable relationships to develop between foreign capital–affiliated semiconductor companies and Japanese semiconductor users. . . . Through the efforts by both sides, foreign capital–affiliated companies and Japanese companies will enjoy long-term prosperity under free competition in the Japanese market.

Is "encourage" the extent to which the Japanese government can influence Japanese industry? What does "long-term relationship" mean? What are the benefits and responsibilities that go along with such a relationship? What does "long-term prosperity" mean in terms of profits?

The crux of the debate between the Japanese and the U.S. governments remains whether the statement about the 20-percent market share constitutes a commitment by the Japanese government. How binding is this recognition of the 20-percent market share expectation? Also hotly debated has been the very existence of this side letter. What does this debate tell us about how the Japanese operate?

It shows that seemingly simple English expressions can be a source of misunderstanding when applied to culture-specific business practices. Without understanding some of these concepts, American businesspeople have as frustrating a time penetrating the Japanese market as government officials had in negotiating and enforcing this side letter.

Most readers would agree that the cultural distance between the United States and Europe is relatively small; the languages and religions are either the same or related. Indeed, Americans doing business in Europe report far fewer cultural problems than do those doing business in Japan. Within Asia, Americans feel most comfortable with societies that are or have been British colonies, Hong Kong and Singapore. A significant part of the population in these two countries can speak English; Singapore, in particular, is a heterogeneous society that is racially and religiously integrated, a concept Americans are comfortable with. Many Americans have said that doing business in Korea and Taiwan is difficult but easier than doing business in Japan. The major difference between Japan and the other two countries is that Japan is, as we have seen, an island that has not suffered a major invasion for two thousand years. (The Mongols tried several times toward the end of the thirteenth century, but a storm at sea—what the Japanese call *kamikaze,* or "God's wind"—prevented them.) By contrast, Korea has never enjoyed more than one century without some infiltration by a foreign power, from both ends of the peninsula, and has had no choice but to cope with foreign values.

Any foreigner visiting Japan can see the Western influence there. Yet Japan has had the freedom to choose the cultural influences it adopts and how to adapt those to its own needs. Not many countries have had that privilege for over a millennium. At the same time, because of Japan's relative immunity from foreign influence, the key elements of Japanese culture have intensified with the passage of time, and thus little of the Japanese business culture needs to be explicitly stated. Given this history, it is not surprising that among the economically active countries Japan is culturally the furthest from the United States.

WHY THE GAP ISN'T CLOSING

The significant cultural chasm between the United States and Japan has not prompted massive efforts to close that gap. In fact, the opposite seems to have happened. As any organizational expert knows, establishing a good working relationship between two parties requires stabilizing feedback. One party has to provide feedback in the form of explanations and suggestions that prompt behavior change in the other party. Given on a mutual basis, this kind of feedback tends to bring the two parties closer. Unfortunately, the absence of stabilizing feedback significantly hampers U.S.-Japanese relationships.

In a culture where strong traditions have solidified a tacit set of values, norms, and rituals, one would expect the Japanese to take the initiative in explaining their business culture to economic allies. Instead, the Japanese have taken a passive role: most English-language books about Japan are written by Westerners, not by Japanese. When American businesspeople ask their Japanese counterparts why business is done in a particular way or why a particular idea would not work in Japan, they often are given an unsatisfactory response such as, "That's difficult to explain."

There are basically three reasons for this reticence. First, most Japanese have an inadequate knowledge of English, even though they study it in school for many years. Not only do they not practice speaking English, but they do not wish to become too good at it for fear of becoming outcasts in their own society. I have found that businesspeople from the newly industrializing economies speak much better English, mainly because in their societies they get positive reinforcement for speaking English. English, moreover, is a direct language, unlike Japanese, which reinforces ambiguity, an important cultural value in Japan. Excessive clarity is sure to rub someone in Japan the wrong way—hence the difficulty foreigners have in detecting a Japanese *no*. Indeed, there is no direct expression for *no* in the Japanese language. How does one communicate when one cannot easily determine assent or dissent?

Second, the Japanese educational system does not train its students to conceptualize and crystallize abstract thoughts. The American educational system, with its emphasis on two-way interaction, constantly challenges students to verbalize difficult topics concisely. The Japanese system, on the other hand, relies predominantly on one-way lecturing with little feedback and does not provide either students or teachers with much opportunity for interaction. In teaching recent Japanese college graduates in company orientation programs in Japanese, I am continually astounded at how much training they need in articulating their thoughts. Part of the problem here is that the group-oriented nature of the Japanese people works against definitive statements by a single person: in Japan one either does not advance one's opinion publicly or does so with a strong dose of humility.

Third, the Japanese feel that their culture is unique, and that one of the elements of that uniqueness is that foreigners will have difficulty in understanding it. In my extensive travels, I have not yet found a nation that does not feel its culture is unique. But only the Japanese seem to believe this so strongly that they do not try to reach out to the best of their ability.

Thus, the enigma is left for the foreigners to solve. Given the fact that most American businesspeople cannot speak Japanese, much less read and write it, we have the problem of the blind men and the elephant. In that story, one blind man touches the side of the elephant and says that an elephant is like a wall; another touches the foot and says that it is like the trunk of a tree; another feels the tail and likens it to a rope; and so on. In other words, foreigners tend to put together a collage of partial perspectives that lack crucial pieces of information and therefore lead to wrong conclusions about culturally appropriate business decisions across the ocean.

The importance of having a good cultural understanding before taking action is particularly important when the cultural distance is wide, because cultural calibration is difficult. One tends either to overreact or to underreact. Some foreigners in Japan act like the bull in the china shop; others become ultraconservative for fear of insulting someone. Despite these difficulties, reasonable familiarity with the Japanese business culture is becoming a prerequisite to global competitiveness.

SOME QUESTIONS THAT NEED TO BE ANSWERED

While much has been written about U.S.-Japan trade friction, little has been written about the *gaishi,* or foreign firm in Japan, from a businessperson's perspective. No trade negotiation between the United States and Japan would be fruitful unless the *gaishi* produces results within the agreed-upon trade environment. The *gaishi* must do so while satisfying two masters with polar-opposite cultures: the Japanese customer and the American parent corporation. Thus, in order truly to understand the challenge a *gaishi* faces, one must understand both the customer's perspective and the perspective of the parent corporation, and relate this to the contribution the *gaishi* makes to the competitiveness of the parent.

The premises of this book are that competing in the Japanese market is critical to competing in worldwide markets; and that before one can compete successfully in the Japanese market, one must have some understanding of differences in culture and business practices. In my first two chapters, I describe some of these differences in relation to these questions: (1) Are Japanese customers fair? (2) How deeply does a foreign firm have to penetrate the Japanese business environment in order to be strategically and tactically successful? In the following four chapters, I discuss the question, "What are the biggest asymmetric difficulties in doing business in Japan?"—an asymmetric difficulty being defined as a cross-cultural challenge more difficult for the American businessperson in Japan than for the Japanese businessperson in the United States. The topics discussed include corporate commitment, marketing, operations, and human resource management. In the final two chapters, I reconsider the concepts of competing with the Japanese in the contexts of partnering and competing in the American market.

I should add a few caveats. First, when I use the expression "the Japanese" or "Japanese businesspeople," I do not mean that all Japanese are alike, any more than all Americans are. Cultural patterns do exist, however, and I have used the Pacific Ocean as a dividing line.

The second word of caution is that I have tried to discuss issues clearly, leading in some instances to descriptions that may sound too extreme. Shades of gray are difficult to distinguish between and even more difficult to understand clearly. For example, when I mention that the Japanese business environment is more tightly coupled than its American counterpart, I do not mean that no elements of the American business scene qualify for that description.

This book provides, as I have said, a perspective from the streets, from one who has experienced business on both sides of the Pacific and who can look at the cultural problem objectively. In this respect, I should like to add a special remark. Amidst the emotional climate surrounding U.S.-Japan trade relations, it is difficult to be open and not be labeled a Japan or America basher. My thinking regarding this matter is simple: having traveled extensively, I can say with certainty that, viewed from an international standpoint, every national culture has both strengths and weaknesses. The United States and Japan are no exceptions, as this book makes clear. I have tried to minimize passing judgment on either nation's business practices, and any positive or negative comments of mine only reflect this general truth. My hope is that this book will contribute to the success of American business in Japan and, as a result, foster global competitiveness. I believe that a stronger America is better for all countries, even Japan.

1

Are Japanese Customers Fair?

THE SUPERMARKET CONCEPT came to Japan from the United States, but the Japanese have adapted it to their own environment by developing their own operating philosophy. A visit to a typical supermarket provides clues to the nature of the Japanese customer and what it means to do business in Japan.

As we enter the store, we are struck by its cleanliness. The floors are spotless, and the goods are arranged on the shelves in orderly fashion. In the produce department, the fruits and vegetables are flawless; no irregularities mar the skin, and a humidifier in the cooler keeps the produce looking fresh. The seafood department has similar appeal. Because of the extremely efficient delivery system and the short distances from sea to market, many of the fish displayed were caught earlier in the day. For the connoisseur who wants guaranteed freshness, there is the *ikesu*, a tank in which live fish are swimming.

It is now 5:30, or a half hour before closing time, and a scene unknown to American shoppers begins. A man clad in a white uniform and wielding a red marker goes

1

through the various fresh foods sections, followed by crowds of housewives. He is the price hatchet man. Until closing time, he monitors the produce he must sell that day, and slashes prices in stages until all is sold. Sometimes aggressive housewives bring him items they want marked down, and he is often accommodating.

Our tour of the store now takes us to the section that sells kitchenware and appliances, such as microwave ovens and compact bread-baking machines. All the appliances are small in comparison with their American counterparts, and American brand names are conspicuous by their absence.

Heading for the checkout counter, we note that despite the last-minute rush, the checkout lines are short. There are fifteen to twenty registers, all open. Ahead of us, a customer who had purchased an appliance has brought it back to complain that it had a small nick and was hard to use. The cashier offers him the choice of a replacement or a refund, no questions asked. This return transaction is not allowed to hold us up; the cashier lets us pay and go through. As we leave, it is five minutes past closing time, but a customer who wishes to come in and make a quick purchase is being admitted.

ANSHINKAN AND QCDS

The experience of visiting the Japanese supermarket can be summarized by the term *anshinkan*. This concept was given new emphasis some years ago by Motoyoshi Shimada, president of Ryoyo Electric, the largest semiconductor distributor in Japan. *Anshinkan* literally means "peace of mind." Everything about the supermarket is designed to reassure the customer that the store is reliable and trustworthy: its goods are fresh and of high quality, its operations are efficient and convenient, and its service is accommodating. The customer is left with the perception that his or her needs will be satisfied.

More concretely, four separate factors contribute to this perception: quality, cost/price, delivery, and service, or QCDS. Of course, these factors are important anywhere in the world. One must have the right product for the customer's need; the quality of that product must be acceptable; the price must be competitive; and delivery and service must conform to the customer's needs. What is notable is how the Japanese perceive each of these factors. My own view, based on having lived more than a decade each in Japan and in the United States, is that there are crucial differences that must be understood by anyone hoping to do business in Japan. One cannot be effective in a market if one does not have a clear picture of what the customer expects.

The different consumer expectations in the United States and Japan are closely tied to the two cultures. Japanese consumers simply demand stricter enforcement of QCDS, and usually get it from their suppliers. The power of the consumer depends to a large extent on the competitive dynamics of a particular industry, but the quality and the service provided by American manufacturers often are inadequate compared with those of their Japanese counterparts. Subcontractors in newly industrialized countries, such as Taiwan and Korea, who work with both American and Japanese firms report that Japanese firms are much more demanding about specifications and quality, and that they could not send to Japan merchandise they are currently supplying to the United States. For example, W. W. Doctor, a general manager of Chung Shing Textile Company, Taiwan's fourth largest textile producer, says, "There is no doubt that if we were to bring the very same apparel produced for sale in America to Japan, at least half could be rejected as defective." Even Americans on temporary assignment in Japan often express their dissatisfaction with American service after they return to the United States.

Certain cultural elements help explain why Japanese consumers enforce QCDS more strictly than do their American counterparts. First and foremost is the principle that the late Konosuke Matsushita, founder of Matsushita Electric Industrial, expressed as "The customer is God." This notion reflects the class structure that prevailed in Japan in the days of the shoguns. The hierarchy, from top down, was *shi-noh-koh-sho,* or "warrior, farmer, craftsman, and merchant." Thus, in Japan the merchant occupies a lower position than the customer. One American businessman was startled by the reaction he received when in his presentation to a Japanese customer he expressed the desire to forge a supplier-customer partnership. In a rare display of emotion, the senior Japanese manager angrily accused the American of trying to get on an equal footing with the customer.

Because of the clear difference in position between seller and buyer, a culture has emerged in Japan that simply will not tolerate anything less than the best the seller can possibly afford. This means that there is no such thing as a loose commitment, as one American executive learned when he was asked by the manager of a Japanese company he supplied whether he could help them find a distribution channel for their products in the United States market. The American said, "I think we could. Let me look into it." Two months later, the Japanese subsidiary of the American firm received an inquiry from the Japanese customer, who had already set up a task force to act upon the American executive's advice. When the American said that he had merely stated he would look into it, but had not yet done so, they were amazed.

Another aspect of business in Japan that tends to spur the seller to the best effort possible is ambiguous feedback. Japanese purchasers never offer the slightest hint of an implied commitment to buy. American businesspeople, who are more inclined to think in the short term, constantly try to learn how much business they can expect if the Japanese customer's special needs are satisfied. They almost never get a clear answer. In a culture that lacks an expression for the concept of *no,* where a Tokyo supplier has a hard time understanding the reactions of an Osaka or Nagoya buyer, it is not surprising that the foreign businessperson cannot elicit such a response.

One aspect of Japanese society that impresses even its harshest critics is how well things work as they are supposed to. Commuter trains run precisely according to the timetable despite the morning rush. Tokyo has never suffered a major blackout, and there has been no major accident on the bullet train in the twenty-six years of its operation. Of course, in a crowded country, the consequences of product failure could be much more dramatic and affect many more people than in the United States. On the expressways in Tokyo, where there is no room for a shoulder on the roadway, one stalled car can back up traffic for miles—in itself enough to require that Japanese

5

cars be reliable. In such a society, suppliers are held to their word, and when something does go wrong, pandemonium strikes.

One distinguishing feature of Japanese institutional customers is their extremely long memories. Organizations in Japan tend to be stable, with permanent employees who have been around for a long time. The record of suppliers who have caused trouble in the past is widely known. Recently I visited a number of Japanese customers with a group of American managers. The Americans were surprised to hear the Japanese bringing up problems that had occurred five years before, problems that the present group of managers had had nothing to do with.

These are some of the business factors that lead to the strict enforcement of QCDS as a whole. Let us now look more closely at the four components of QCDS to see how the differences in perception manifest themselves.

Quality

In our visit to the supermarket, we saw close attention paid to the appearance of the products on display. An American might wonder why it makes a difference when little irregularities appear on the skin of a tangerine—one peels it off anyway. But that's not the way the Japanese feel about it. Products that have the slightest cosmetic defect are either not accepted in the first place or thrown away as nonsalable; they are not offered for sale even as discount merchandise. While people all over the world would, given a choice, desire products that look perfect, the Japanese are especially fanatical about it. Koreans, for example, are, like Americans, much less picky about the outside appearance of a product than the Japanese are. The Korean expression *koenchanayo,* meaning "That's about right," typifies this philosophy. The Japanese reaction would be, "Close but no cigar." A Japanese executive once told me that a power-plant controller produced by his firm had been rejected by the government because of a small nick in the outside casing. Since everyone knows that a small nick has nothing to do with how well the product works—in fact, the controller had passed the functional tests without a hitch—what was the problem?

The Japanese view is that cosmetic anomalies are an indication of something wrong in the manufacturing process that could lead to more serious problems. For the Japanese, the outside appearance is an important indicator of *anshinkan.* I once mustered enough courage to ask an MIT professor why his office was not in order. His answer made perfect sense from a U.S. perspective: he had better things to do with his time. And, in fact, there are professors all over America who have untidy offices and yet produce excellent academic work. In Japan, however, the perception is that the occupant of an untidy desk cannot think clearly; such a person's mind must be as disorganized as his or her desk. Japanese customers like to visit their suppliers' plants, and a dirty plant almost always leads to skepticism about the quality of the plant's output. To the Japanese, *anshinkan* in the output is *anshinkan* in the process.

Another aspect of quality that tends to be perceived differently in the United States and Japan is the need for a period of "shakedown." Many American products have good reliability, particularly durability, but only after they have gone through an early period of erratic and unreliable performance. In contrast, many Japanese products give no problems whatsoever in their early life but prove less durable than their U.S. counterparts, in part because of cost consciousness in the use of parts. When I lived in the United States, an American friend once jokingly advised me to buy a used car with about ten thousand miles on it because by that point the early problems would already have been taken care of. As it happened, I did buy an American car with ten thousand miles on it, and although the previous owner told me he had had to fix the car a number of times, I drove the car without a problem for the next forty thousand miles.

While one must balance minimization of early difficulties with maximization of long-term reliability, the former often provides more leverage in terms of the market reputation of the product. Early failure has much greater negative impact on sales than a problem many years later in the life of the product. The Japanese consider early failure to be a sign of poor long-term reliability. The fact that this assumption may not be scientifically accurate is irrelevant; perceptions influence buying decisions.

Despite the stringent quality controls Japanese manufacturers impose on their operations, even they have not attained zero defects. Occasionally a product malfunctions, and when that happens, the Japanese are unforgiving. One bad experience with a product is enough to close a Japanese customer's mind for several purchase cycles. In those cases where the supplier is given a second chance—perhaps because the customer is dependent on the product—the response must be timely, the failure must have been thoroughly analyzed, and satisfactory corrective action must be provided for all subsequent products delivered to that customer. That's easy to say, hard to do. In Japan, the industrial customer is not satisfied solely with a manufacturer replacing the defective product with a functioning product.

Cost

It may not be obvious from looking at price levels in Tokyo that enormous cost pressure is put on manufacturers. After all, market prices in many product categories are sky-high, giving rise to the discussions in the structural impediment talks concerning pricing differentials between the United States and Japan. Recently one of my friends from New York asked me to take him to the discount camera store section of Tokyo to see whether he could buy a Japanese camera accessory at about 10 percent lower than back home. When we went there, I negotiated with a store manager, whose reaction was, "Beat New York pricing on Japanese camera goods? No way!"

If a manufacturer could capture such high prices, it's natural to think either there is considerable profit built in or one's product costs are too high. Neither is the case. To begin with, while generalizations are hard to make, it is often said that the ratio of retail price to manufacturer price tends to be around 1.7 in America, while the analogous number in Japan is 3.0. This is consistent with what I hear in the Japanese electronics industry: that the manufacturer's cost must be less than one-third of the list price.

This means that the mark-ups at the distribution level

tend to be much higher in Japan. Several factors contribute to this. First, real estate costs are much higher, particularly in Tokyo. Second, the ingrained, multitier distribution channels in Japan and the philosophy of *kamaseru* ("allow participation") bias society toward full employment in the distribution sector over distribution efficiency. Third, the personalized service the Japanese market demands often requires considerable staffing, which nowadays, at wages equivalent to or higher than their American counterparts, is costly.

Thus, for Japanese consumers, who have limited disposable income after paying rent, to be able to buy products at barely tolerable prices, and for Japanese manufacturers to satisfy their relatively loyal distribution channels, product costs must be kept at an absolute minimum. The fact that Japanese goods must be priced competitively in export markets further drives Japanese cost consciousness.

Everywhere in the world, Japanese consumers have a harsh view of price increases. As a result, one way Japanese manufacturers increase margins is by bringing out products with new features. In markets where price declines occur fairly rapidly, new-product development cycles tend to be shorter in order to keep margins at reasonable levels.

In industrial goods, the Japanese resist explicit price increases because of *anshinkan*. The customer who in turn is a manufacturer of another product will have worked the cost of a purchased part into the price structure of the final product. Given the high distribution mark-up in the Japanese market, product costs must be held at a minimum. If the cost of one part increases, the manufacturer is caught in a real cost bind, unable to pass along the increase because of resistance to price increases. Such a prospect is hardly consistent with *anshinkan*.

Another common phenomenon in Japan is hybrid pricing. Many Japanese customers like one-stop shopping and purchase multiple products as a group from one supplier. Japanese suppliers often bundle different products and services together to meet this need and later work out the profitability allocation to various divisions within their own organization. This practice is called *donburi kanjo* ("calculation within one bucket"). Foreign affiliate firms, on the other hand, often price on a line-item basis because several divisions back in the United States authorize pricing independently and no one wants to be at a price disadvantage relative to another division.

A particularly interesting example of this tactic is pricing for the service guarantee that accompanies a product. One aspect of *anshinkan* is that service for a product is provided without strings attached. In American industries when the warranty period is over, the customer often is charged separately for service. In Japan the notion predominates that the product is supposed to work even after the initial warranty period, and at the very least, minor problems are taken care of without additional payment.

Delivery

Japanese businesses are constantly trying to reduce the time required to move things around. This is true of U.S. businesses as well, but because of the smaller land mass of Japan, people there seem to expect even faster delivery.

One of Konosuke Matsushita's rules of retailing says that it is clearly the store's fault if a product that a customer desires is out of stock; that the store should apologize to the customer, regardless of the reason; and that it should deliver the product to the customer as soon as possible. Too many American stores tend to take a matter-of-fact attitude when something is not available.

Moreover, the dictum that there are no loose commitments in Japan is nowhere more true than in its application to delivery dates. Meeting delivery dates is, of course, easier said than done. A host of problems can cause such commitments to slip: manufacturing can encounter a snag, products can be allocated to other sales regions, mistakes can be made in paperwork, and delivery systems can break down. But in a competitive environment the customer will not tolerate any of these excuses.

In Japan, when a change in a delivery schedule is inevitable, a personal visit by a responsible person in management is required. Neither a letter nor a phone call is sufficient. The Japanese culture values the concern shown by a personal visit, with an explanation for the failure to deliver and an assurance that the best efforts are being exerted to minimize the delay. The logic that says, "We can't do anything about this anyway, so we'll call them or send them a form letter" creates a negative impression.

I once purchased clothing from a Japanese department store a week before Christmas, with the understanding that the clothes would be delivered before Christmas Day. The goods did not arrive; and when I called the store, I was told that an error in paperwork had been made and would be corrected right away. The next day a manager showed up on my doorstep not only with the clothing but with a beautifully wrapped box of cookies and profuse apologies. By contrast, when a bed purchased from a well-known department store in the United States failed to arrive on the day promised, not only were there no apologies but I was made to feel that I should sympathize with the store's hectic delivery schedule.

The first step, then, is to meet one's own delivery commitments. The second step is to match deliveries precisely to the customer's need for the merchandise. One way to do this is to make sure that the product is in stock so that it is always available to the customer. In Toyama, where a number of pharmaceutical firms are located, salespeople provide a special service, visiting each home and filling the first-aid boxes with medicine. The customers pay only for the amount they have used; the inventory cost is on the company. In the industrial arena, a stringent expectation is just-in-time delivery. In order to avoid having to carry inventory, a customer specifies a fifteen-minute period during which merchandise will be accepted. Often this strict requirement means that the supplier's truck leaves early to allow for possible traffic congestion, and must circle the block until the specified time period. Remember, "The customer is God."

Service

Manufacturing firms as well as service firms compete through the service they provide. My perception, based on many crossings of the Pacific, is that while the service provided by the best American firms is comparable with that of the best Japanese firms, the U.S. average is abominable compared with that of Japan.

One of Konosuke Matsushita's rules says, "When a customer comes back to the store for an exchange or return, deal with him or her even more pleasantly than when the original purchase was made." Recall that in our visit to a Japanese supermarket a customer returned an appliance without argument. At the same time, that transaction did not delay us; we paid for our merchandise and left, and as we did so, another customer was permitted to enter after the store had closed. That's service.

By contrast, more times than I care to remember I have arrived at an American store and brought my purchases to the checkout counter shortly before closing only to be told that the register had been turned off and that I should return the next day. Similarly, the American customer often is expected to be tolerant of poor service when the system is overloaded; waiting lines are poorly managed, waiters bring the wrong food and disappear when they are needed—the list could go on and on. In Japan a customer seldom has to put up with compromised service because of overload. Most Japanese who have traveled to the United States have a relatively poor impression of American service, although they are too polite to say so to most Americans.

The point is not that all American firms give poor service, but that, unfortunately, many do. And I have no sympathy for these firms when they complain that the Japanese market is unfair to them. They need to correct their basic service, instead of trying to export poor service using the government's crowbar.

There are several levels to Japanese-style service. The

most basic is meeting one's commitments as advertised and stated. Many American firms try to guarantee this level of service through the use of systematized operating procedures: they define every important service-related activity, train employees to deal with customers, and measure their performance against standardized criteria.

In Japan basic service means, first of all, that the customer is never wrong. To quote Matsushita again, "Think of customer complaints as the voice of God and accept them." Even a customer's misuse of a product is seldom considered an excuse for not fixing the problem; it is the firm's responsibility to make sure that the customer knows how to use the product. The manner in which customer complaints are handled is also noteworthy. Whereas the customer in the United States often is referred from one person to another, in Japan the philosophy is that everyone represents the firm: the first person who hears about the problem must take total responsibility for dealing with the customer, even if some other department eventually becomes involved.

The second level of service is meeting the customer's needs as the customer sees them. This level of service is more difficult to accomplish because the system may make it impossible to control. For example, at a checkout counter in an American store, the employee ringing up the sales is generally working on a first in—first out basis. If the person ahead of me in line is paying by check and the cashier must wait for the check to be authorized, I must wait until that transaction is completed, even if it takes several minutes and my one or two purchases will take ten seconds at most, because the point-of-sale system does not allow parallel operations. Even if there were a way around

15

this problem which would allow the next customer to be served before the previous transaction has been completed, there might not be much incentive to use it, particularly for a cashier paid by the hour. The Japanese philosophy is expressed as *komawari ga kiku,* which means turning requests around quickly without exercising the whole organizational bureaucracy of the supplier.

The third level of service, and the most difficult for a foreign company, is the kind that fulfills the unstated needs of the customer. There is a Japanese concept called *kikubari,* which means being extremely sensitive to other people's concerns and needs and thus responding to the unstated. It is clearly an integral part of Japanese society; some years ago a book called *Kikubari no Susume (May I Suggest* Kikubari?) by Kenji Suzuki became a nationwide bestseller. Applied to business, *kikubari* requires not only selling a product or service but doing whatever is necessary to help the customer solve his or her problems and feel good. This may mean introducing the customer to someone who can help solve a problem that has little to do with the product or service in question. On a more simple level, it often means throwing in something for free. Matsushita says, "A giveaway, even if it is one piece of paper, will always make the customer happy."

This is not to say that no American firms provide excellent service. United Airlines's Mileage Plus program tries to ensure that the most frequent travelers get the most benefits, including free upgrades and travel. The important point is that this service is administered by a computer system that tracks registered flight miles and can display the information to any of the airline's ground crew. This system is superior to anything I've seen by a Japanese carrier. However, travelers do disagree about the level of personalized service one encounters in the flight itself, where service depends more on the individual initiative of cabin attendants than on a computer system.

. . .

The preceding description of QCDS may not sound necessarily Japanese; the best American firms do much the same. But if the QCDS performance of American firms in Japan is a measure of the degree to which they do, too few are practicing it effectively. QCDS constitutes a set of basic criteria for competition worldwide. The Japanese culture and tradition enforce the strictest observance of these criteria. It is my strong feeling that the Japanese are justified in demanding professionalism from their suppliers with respect to QCDS.

BEYOND QCDS: OTHER BARRIERS TO SURMOUNT

If foreign firms in general came closer to meeting the QCDS expectations of the Japanese customer, I am convinced that they would be doing far more business in Japan. On the other hand, some aspects of *anshinkan* go beyond simple QCDS and make life extremely difficult for the foreign businessperson. To the extent that Japanese purchasers demand this level of *anshinkan,* I believe they will find it a luxury the world will not allow them, much as the world did not allow Americans the luxury of unlimited supplies of cheap oil for their gas-guzzling automobiles.

Some of the excessive *anshinkan*-related expectations come from the fact that Japan is an island country. Recall that having had no sizable military or business invasion for the last two thousand years, the Japanese have culturally had it their way. On the other hand, in neighboring Korea, where stability has never lasted more than a century throughout its history, the analogous term for *anshin* or *anshim* is heard much less frequently.

Let us look at some aspects of Japanese *anshinkan* that could be thought of as excessive.

Product-Related Barriers

On the one hand, the Japanese are totally justified in asking for products that fit their needs. Appliances that are designed for roomy American homes, and that do not fit into small Japanese houses, deserve not to sell in the Japanese market. Products that do not conform to the general aesthetic desires of the Japanese can succeed only to the extent that the difference is perceived as a curiosity—and, in fact, there are such success stories.

On the other hand, the demands of the Japanese market tend to become excessive when customers insist on their cultural uniqueness and reject foreign products that would meet their needs just as well as their own. One example of this is the Japanese tendency to refuse to join international standards. In personal computers, for example, IBM did an excellent job of establishing a standard that led to explosive market expansion in the early 1980s. Although standardization leads to efficiency and ease in interfacing and communication, the Japanese use their own specifications for the domestic market, not only making it difficult for foreign manufacturers to penetrate the Japanese market but creating problems when companies with extensive international operations wish to standardize their computers worldwide.

A related tendency is what might be called the "not manufactured here" syndrome. The Japanese tend to distrust products not made in Japan. This bias dates back to the years right after the Second World War, when Japan was a poor country and believed that its only hope for survival lay in buying as few materials as possible and adding the most value possible. This mentality, still vivid in the minds of Japanese senior managers who lived through the poverty-stricken years, has led to the concept of *jimaeshugi,* which means making as much as possible internally rather than acquiring parts, tools, and capabilities from abroad. In the West, the decision whether to make or to buy subassemblies that go into a product is usually economic: if the final product is produced in large numbers, it may pay to make the subassembly internally, but if the volume is low, it may make sense to purchase the parts from the outside. One American executive was quoted in *Electronics Buyers News,* a trade journal, as saying, "We don't make what we can buy. It's that simple. The results are improved pricing and enhanced profitability for the company." In Japan, however, the bias is toward making everything, even in uneconomical quantities. I once asked an executive of a Japanese electronics firm how it could justify designing, fabricating, and assembling a printed circuit board in quantities of only a couple of dozen a month. From an economic standpoint, the practice made no sense, but the firm insisted upon it for reasons of *anshinkan.* First, the firm did not have to depend upon a supplier; by manufacturing the board itself, the firm could guarantee its availability. Second, it kept the manufacturing know-how within the firm and did not have to worry about leakage. Finally, by retaining control over every aspect of the manufacturing operation, the firm could solve customers' problems quickly, thus providing *anshinkan* to its customers. When confronted with a cost argument, the Japanese almost always limit their calculations to the cost of individual parts; seldom do they include development, depreciation, and other intangible costs.

The impetus for *jimaeshugi* among the Japanese dates back to the Meiji Restoration. Japan's lack of technology at that time made its economy and military humiliatingly inferior to those of the West. Determined never to repeat this mistake, Japan has been on a technology accumulation treadmill ever since. This has involved many methods: licensing technology from willing foreign firms; scanning every available piece of industrial information from the West and improving it for the Japanese business environment; making value-added products at home rather than buying from foreign countries; only reluctantly transferring technology abroad; and more recently, developing new technology. In a number of strategic, standardized product categories, including cameras, compact cars, consumer electronics, semiconductors, and computer systems, Japan is now the only country that can independently develop and produce new products from raw materials alone. The United States, along with nearly all the industrial nations of the world, depends on Japanese components and equipment technology.

Thus, it is wrong to assume that in strategic, high-technology industries, the Japanese do not aggressively import manufactured goods primarily in order to build up a massive trade surplus. The truth is more threatening: even as the Japanese display support for *sogo izon* (mutual dependency), they insist on what Peter Drucker calls "adversarial trade," out of a refusal ever again to become significantly dependent on foreign technology. This paradoxical stance leads to contradictory situations. Thus, before the ink was dry on the U.S.-Japanese supercomputer agreement of March 1990, which supposedly aimed to promote the purchase of foreign supercomputers by Japan, MITI announced a joint government–private sector project to develop Japanese parallel supercomputers. The facts were simple: Japanese electronics firms trailed behind their American counterparts in this field, one crucial to scientific research, and technological dependence on the United States could not be permitted. In Japanese high-technology thinking, free trade takes a back seat to winning the technology accumulation war.

These product-related tendencies are, I believe, beginning to change. Some individual and institutional customers in Japan are trying aggressively to acquire foreign products as well as parts, subassemblies, and tools. Such customers are still too few, however; and although it is unfortunate, it is perhaps necessary that the U.S. government put pressure on the Japanese Ministry of International Trade and Industry, and that it in turn does so on Japanese private industry to force a change in these biases. For example, as a result of the 1986 Semiconductor Agreement, large Japanese electronics firms have had to report to MITI on how they will achieve an increase in the foreign supplier's share of their semiconductor purchases.

Process-Related Barriers

A second area of frustration for American businesspeople is the marketing process itself. In Japan it takes much longer to break into a market than in the United States, and return in the form of sales comes much later and in smaller quantities. Several factors contribute to this situation.

One difference between selling in the United States and selling in Japan is that the sales process in Japan is human-intensive rather than product-intensive. The difference derives from the basis on which the customer differentiates between suppliers. In the United States, products and services tend to be strongly differentiated. The greater the competitive advantage of a product or a service, the less depends on the salesperson's skill. A customer who really wants a given product will, if necessary, deal with an unpleasant salesperson in order to obtain it.

The Japanese, on the other hand, will not as a rule buy even a desired product from a salesperson who in any way offends them. For many years similar products were offered by competing manufacturers, and human relations therefore became the important differentiating element. In some industries in Japan, the frequency with which a salesperson meets with the customer correlates fairly closely with the amount of business the salesperson receives. Some companies even purchase a less-than-optimal product in order to maintain a relationship with someone they trust, provided there is a good track record with respect to QCDS. In such cases, QCDS is a necessary but not sufficient condition.

Another factor frequently at issue in buying decisions

in Japan is the location of the factory where the product is made. There is a strong preference for a local factory, and again *anshinkan* plays an important role. Japanese customers derive a great deal of *anshinkan* from being able to talk with the engineers who have developed a product and to see products being manufactured and in inventory. The *anshinkan* goes deeper, however. In Japan, everyone except foreigners is registered in the *koseki* system, which records crucial information regarding family and history. The system not only keeps track of people but keeps them from running away if they do something wrong. Sales subsidiaries of foreign firms are not perceived as being anchored in Japan to the point where they will not run away. A significant investment in a local plant or some other major financial commitment constitutes some assurance of permanence or stability.

Japanese purchasing agents do not offer these reasons for requesting a local factory. They prefer to comment that a local factory would reduce the turnaround time for service, for example. Such a reason is valid in itself, but the age of globalization does not tolerate excessive *anshinkan*.

Japanese customers demand a level of consistency and continuity from their suppliers that is sometimes justified but often excessive. Once Japanese manufacturers begin a certain product line, they do not under normal circumstances abandon it. This attitude often poses a problem for proposed partnerships between American and Japanese firms, when the potential Japanese partner is unwilling to terminate an inefficient business. Sony Corporation agonized before announcing that it would change from the Beta VCR format it had developed to the VHS format which had become the mainstream, and Sony still manufactures Beta-formatted tapes and VCRs because it feels responsible to loyal Beta users. By contrast, much American business culture thrives on change, and changes in product line and support plans are frequent. In the future, the quickening pace of technology will force the Japanese customer to stop clinging to old decisions; but for now, every time an American firm changes its mind the Japanese customer tends to subtract points on the *anshinkan* scorecard.

For the newcomer to the Japanese market, the barriers are especially difficult to overcome. In the United States, unless the competition's customer penetration is thorough, a certain amount of price-cutting will attract attention and perhaps even stimulate sales. If one can't buy one's way into the business, how else can one get in? After all, one definition of a free market with price elasticity is that some price exists at which the customer will show interest; and that the lower the price, the more the customer will buy.

Of course, Japanese customers also prefer suppliers who provide the best value for the money. The Japanese often claim, however, that one cannot tell whether going with a new supplier will yield the best value for the money until one builds some experience with that supplier. Suppose a customer places a significant order with a supplier who offers a price considerably lower than the present supplier's. But then let us say that a quality problem surfaces and the response from the manufacturer is slow. The Japanese purchasing manager would probably say that the cost of going to the new entrant was higher than that of staying with the former vendor. Moreover, the customer might have irritated the former vendor and find that good service is no longer available from that company. Of course, in the long term, if the new supplier is given another chance and recovers, more orders could gradually be placed with that supplier. One Japanese executive I spoke with called this a "long-term free market."

In other words, it is not impossible for a newcomer to break into the Japanese market, but it is very difficult. An executive of a Japanese semiconductor manufacturer once told me that a new supplier is forced to provide dirt-cheap pricing but gets only a token order that in no way justifies the upfront service the customer demands. Gradually the size of the orders increases; and with luck, after two years the manufacturer can start to make money from that customer.

Often the person within the customer organization who crusades most aggressively for the non-Japanese supplier is the harshest critic of that supplier in front of management and sales staff. In many Japanese organizations, employees are judged by the mistakes they make in the course of their careers rather than by their accomplishments. In such an environment, it is safer to continue to deal with the present supplier than to switch to a new one and become the target of finger-pointing when something goes wrong.

Breaking into the Japanese market, then, means several things: first, the product must be better than that offered by Japanese competition; second, inordinate pressure must be put on influential members of the decision-making unit to overcome inertia and conservatism; and third, QCDS must be immaculate—better, in fact, than the Japanese competitors' until the supplier relationship strengthens.

This last factor is especially important, because in this conservative environment mistakes can be perceived in totally different ways depending on whether an error is

25

made by an established supplier or a relatively new one. An established supplier may receive a slap on the wrist, and if the best efforts are made for recovery, the customer's organization is sympathetic. A new supplier, however, encounters a barrage of criticism, and the crusader within the organization who promoted the newcomer's selection comes under pressure as well.

.   .   .

A look at the trade friction between the United States and Japan reveals extreme arguments made by people remote from the action. Americans ignore the fact that their QCDS performance may not be satisfactory and put the blame squarely on the unfairness of the Japanese market. Japanese ignore the biases in their market that make it extremely difficult for foreigners to participate in it. Both sides should do their homework. In particular, American firms whose QCDS capabilities need improvement would do well to hone them instead of complaining, for their efforts can only improve their competitive situation both in Japan and in any other world market.

2

Breaking into the Japanese Business Environment

IT IS 7:30 IN THE MORNING, and I have entered Ookayama station to start my commute to work. I head for the vending machines to purchase my ticket, and someone rushes in front of me. I wait until he is finished. As I go through the ticket gates and walk toward the platform, the train schedule indicates that there are trains every two minutes during rush hour; the next train is at 7:32.

The platform is already filled with people, some lined up near the markings on the platform showing where the train doors will open. The train pulls into the station, and my heart sinks when I see that it is packed. I may not be able to get on this one unless a lot of people get off. When the train stops and the doors open next to the lines of waiting commuters, only two passengers emerge. But the people on the platform begin to push, and I am sucked into the train in the pressing crowd. I make it in, but the man behind me is in the way of the closing door. The pushers come and politely say, "Let's work on your shoulders first—one, two, three—and now the knees and legs."

27

He is in the train, and the door closes. The train has been in the station no longer than thirty seconds.

I always board the first car of the train, which lets me off next to the stairs leading to the exit at my stop. Now that I'm in the car, I have people breathing down my neck and in my face. I could let my attaché case go, and it wouldn't fall. It is a hot summer day, but all the windows in the train are closed. Although everyone is sweating, no one tries to let in any air until a Caucasian man finally opens two windows. He has certainly done the right thing, but everyone stares.

As the train slows down at the next station, the passengers standing against the front bulkhead wince in pain at the pressure of the massed people on their rib cages. When the train stops and the door behind me opens, I am pushed out of the train, but I manage to fight my way back in. Fortunately I do not have to repeat this at every station, because the platform is sometimes on the other side of the train. I finally get to my stop. I go through the ticket gates and hand my ticket to the guard. Then I hear him shout, "Mr. Customer! Twenty more yen, please!" I turn around, but it is the person behind me he is calling back, and I go on my way. Quite an exercise just to get to work!

THE JAPANESE BUSINESS ENVIRONMENT

The Japanese business environment is strongly influenced by the physical environment of Japan. As the preceding description illustrates, a great many people live in a small area. A crowded environment leads to much competition:

people compete to buy train tickets, people push to get into trains. They are aggressive.

An American who does not like crowded environments can move elsewhere. The Japanese have no choice. The mere existence in the United States of the word *claustrophobic* indicates a range of environments unavailable in a place like Japan.

A crowded environment does not offer much leeway to those who live in it. There are few wide-open, uncharted opportunities to pursue. In such an environment, it is not enough to be industrious; one must be shrewd to be successful.

For the Japanese, part of being shrewd is learning the rules of the game from those who have experience. In a process that is quite systematized, they actively seek know-how from their seniors in order to avoid making mistakes their predecessors made. At Harvard Business School, I encountered a close-knit community of Japanese students who studied together as a group, using notes left for them by earlier Japanese students. The notes are striking in that they are as much concerned with the format for writing the answers as with their content—a carryover from preparatory schools in Japan, where I found teachers spent a great deal of time explaining the answer formats that graders tended to like.

The same effort is apparent in the industrial context. When pursuing a new opportunity, the Japanese conduct a rigorous study, learning from others as much as they can. American corporations conduct such studies as well, but in the individualistic American culture, managers tend to rely on their own common sense and problem-solving abilities. The Japanese, in addition to drawing on the specific experience of others, have developed excellent pattern-recognition abilities that enable them to spot trends in what they see. This type of applied thinking contrasts with the importance the Koreans put on pure scholarship, which is undoubtedly the result of a strong Confucian influence. For example, Korean firms value Ph.D.'s much more than do their Japanese counterparts, who place a high value on practical work experience within their own firms. Indeed, cultural factors underpin Japan's remarkable catch-up in a number of industries.

As I have noted, the crowded environment of Japan creates intense competition, which makes it difficult to sustain a product advantage for a long period of time; using the strategies just described, someone can catch up quickly. When Domino's Pizza franchises started in Japan, it took three months for three competitors to appear, and within a year there were more than thirty. The Japanese business environment therefore drives its participants to create barriers to competition in the form of entities that tend to last somewhat longer than product advantages or market-segment advantages. This tendency, of course, makes it difficult for foreigners to break into the Japanese business environment.

TIGHT COUPLING AND THE MEANING OF INSIDERSHIP

Japan is what an engineer might call a tightly coupled society, meaning it is closely knit; information is readily available to those within the system and can be obtained efficiently. Rumors travel rapidly, and secrets are hard to keep. Such a system fosters considerable interdependency among the government, academia, and the private sector. In a way, Japanese society is less private than Western society; trust and reputation are an important part of getting anything done. Perhaps it is natural for Japan to be tightly coupled: the land mass is small, distances are short, the people are relatively homogeneous, and centuries of isolation have solidified its insular nature. In any case, tight coupling has produced good results in the efficiency and harmony of team endeavors.

By contrast, the United States is loosely coupled. The land mass is large, and distances are great. People like their privacy, and thoughts and possessions are not readily shared. In the governmental system of checks and balances, each branch of government keeps the others in line. The government, academia, and the private sector interact at arm's length, in a confrontational mode. Any proposal for setting up a U.S. department of international trade and industry similar to MITI, the ministry that drives Japanese industrial policy, is opposed with the argument that such a unified power would be dangerous. It is important, however, for Americans to understand how the tight links within Japanese society affect the business environment.

American executives often complain about the unfair barrier that keeps Americans from becoming insiders in Japan. In order to see whether this complaint is justified, we must first see what it means to be an insider in Japan.

To begin with, being an insider in the Japanese business environment is not a necessary condition for doing business successfully in Japan. One cannot be a total outsider, however. As I shall discuss later in this chapter, being what I call a semi-insider is the key. Many newer Japanese firms who are not total insiders have a respectable market share and profitability.

Being an insider in Japan entails a responsibility and a loss of freedom that might be unacceptable to a foreign firm. Insider status means being tied to an interdependent system of four distinct stakeholders in Japanese society: *sei, kan, zai,* and *gaku,* or politicians, bureaucrats, industry, and academia, respectively. Let me look first at the triangular relationship among the first three of these groups.

The Connections among Politicians, Bureaucrats, and Industry

Being an insider is generally discussed in terms of being a member of the group; little is said about the financial requirements of total insidership. Yet in Japan, as in America, politicians need votes and money. Votes are earned through bureaucratic regulations that favor industry. The money comes from industry in the form of political contributions and "party tickets" to fundraisers, which also constitute political contributions. Regulations limiting the amount and form of political contributions have been set up to prevent politicians from being bought out, but industry is becoming ever more creative in finding ways to make such donations. In Japan politicians need inflated budgets to meet heavy social obligations such as weddings and funerals; a recent study by NHK (Japan Broadcasting Corporation) found that the average politician was spending between half a million and one million dollars a year. If politicians need the money and firms are willing to give it, a way will be found. A foreign firm that is not ready to be part of this activity is not going to come close to being an insider.

Similarly, the Keidanren, the most prestigious industry association in Japan, has close relationships with politicians, and organizing contributions to political parties is one of its most important functions. A firm that wishes to join the association for purposes of public visibility must be able to afford to make such contributions.

The bureaucracy also plays a give-and-take game. The ministers are appointed by negotiations between the prime minister and the leaders of the various factions of the Liberal Democratic Party. Needless to say, the ministries have a significant influence on industry through the regulations they initiate and enforce. To establish connections with the ministries, industry hires retired bureaucrats at high salaries in a practice known as *amakudari* ("descent from heaven"). NHK recently reported that some *amakudari* bureaucrats collected millions of dollars in severance pay after only five years of working in industry.

The Connections among Bureaucrats, Industry, and Academia

Of a somewhat different nature is the triangular relationship among the latter three of the four groups of stakeholders: the bureaucrats, industry, and academia. It is clear that, for better or worse, the Japanese government has steered industry toward endeavors it has deemed of strategic importance, through the concept of strategic industry. Typically, in a joint project of government, academia, and business, the government takes the initiative, although it may choose whether to fund the project. It lines up both a renowned professor in the field and the industrial association to which most of the major industry participants belong. Together the professor and the association set up the project and execute it. Recent examples include the VLSI (Very Large Scale Integration) project, which gave Japanese semiconductor manufacturers a sizable advantage in the dynamic memory race; the Fifth Generation Project, aimed at developing artificial intelligence technology; the Sigma project, set up to put together an engineering workstation environment for increasing the productivity of developing electronics applications; and TRON, designed to establish a Japanese standard for operating systems and microprocessors. In the case of TRON, MITI claims it is not involved in the project. It is no coincidence that these examples cover the most important areas of the information industries. MITI's vision is to infuse a high degree of technology and knowledge intensity into Japan's industrial composition.

The concept of strategic industry has worked with varying success, including some notable failures. The success of such a cooperative venture depends in part on what is known as the coalition game. A coalition will hold together only as long as the benefits of group activity outweigh the cost of participation for individual members. In the case of the VLSI project, the cooperative venture succeeded because the participants were uniformly lagging behind the state of the art and the potential gain for each was large; projects in which participating firms have had differing levels of capability have not pulled together as well.

Another factor that contributes to the success of cooperative ventures is the mutual familiarity of the members. An industry representative might be a former student of the professor in charge. Participants from competing companies might have been classmates or might have worked together on other projects organized by the industry association. Industry people have well-established relationships with MITI; they are expected to pay tribute to the ministry by visiting regularly, sharing information about the industry, and engaging in such ceremonial rituals as New Year greetings.

Shidoh

At this point, we must consider another important concept in Japanese business. *Shidoh* means roughly "guidance," and the term "administrative guidance" is regularly used in connection with the enforcement of MITI policies; but, in fact, *shidoh* is far more pervasive than such a term suggests. Some Americans think of guidance as advice; the direct translation of the verb *shidoh* is "to instruct." Both concepts vastly underrate the extent to which *shidoh* in the industrial context acts as an informal control mechanism.

The word *shidoh* is frequently used to describe vertical relationships in Japan. MITI provides *shidoh* to private-sector firms in terms of industrial policy. Large Japanese firms provide *shidoh* to their distribution channels, an intricate concept to be examined in a later chapter. Japanese professors provide *shidoh* to their students with respect to career direction. These relationships, unlike their counterparts in the United States, are all vertical in the sense that the subordinate in the relationship is obliged to follow the superior's *shidoh*. In Japan no one explicitly tells anyone else what to do because that would cause the recipient of the command to lose face, but if the *shidoh* or compulsory volunteering is not followed, there are many ways that the superior can make things difficult for the subordinate. For example, when Japan's trading partners threatened retaliation if its trade surplus did not decrease, MITI changed its stance from promoting exports to promoting imports. In one instance, MITI asked large users of semiconductors to submit a plan for purchasing more semiconductors from foreign firms. Some plans went to the extent of redesigning a product to accommodate use of foreign integrated circuits. In theory, the firms were not required to submit these plans, but MITI's administrative guidance was strong. The power of MITI is considered by some to have decreased over time, but it is still greater than that wielded by the U.S. departments of commerce or defense over the nonmilitary sectors of American industry.

The Japanese culture tends to ensure that *shidoh* is followed. One concept that generally feels awkward to the Westerner, accustomed to either enforcing something or not, is *danryokuteki unei,* literally translated as "flexible enforcement." The Japanese implemented this concept for the six months immediately following the introduction of the sales tax, and almost everyone paid.

Suppose, for example, that a particular firm decides not to follow MITI's *shidoh.* Nothing will happen to it overnight. The next time a steering committee is formed, however, that company might notice a difference in the way it is treated. MITI, along with the various industry associations, is a storehouse of industry intelligence and expertise, and the offending company might subtly be put in a disadvantageous position. Of course, if the *shidoh* is so inappropriate that all affected firms resist, then MITI itself is in trouble.

In the United States, by contrast, the government is not merely loosely coupled to industry but is the frequent source and target of attacks. The Japanese were surprised to see the Commerce Department criticize Sematech, the consortium of American semiconductor manufacturers performing joint research aimed at enhancing their competitive position in world markets. In Japan, such criticism would have shown an absence of government cohesion with industry and a lack of confidence as well. American firms, in turn, often openly criticize the U.S. government's handling of trade policy and negotiations. After all, it is a system of checks and balances, as well as of freedom of speech.

Coupling between Japanese Firms

Shinrai, or trust, is a term heard frequently in Japanese business. It is central to all relationships in Japan, but particularly to lateral relationships, just as *shidoh* is important in vertical ones. At the same time, the Japanese concept of trust is rarely understood by Westerners.

To the American, trust usually means the ability to depend on someone. In marriage it means counting on one's spouse not to be unfaithful; in business it means, among other things, counting on a business partner not to turn around and cooperate with a competitor, even in a different arena.

In Japan the businessperson who thinks of trust in that

fashion is considered naïve. Trust in Japan specifically means that two parties will act in accordance with an agreed-on relationship, and when there is any doubt, they will adhere to the norms of Japanese behavior (*atarimae,* "common sense"). One norm is relativism: nothing is absolute, everything is situational. Under the right circumstances, it is acceptable for a firm to switch alliances. If the spirit of the agreement or the norms of Japanese behavior are violated, however, the offending party ultimately learns that it has crossed the line.

The concept of trust is closely related to the manner in which business arrangements are managed—through contractual wording or personal administration. In a loosely coupled society, litigation is central to the arbitration of disputes between people of widely differing beliefs and values. A tightly coupled, homogeneous society like Japan has far less need for a formal adjudication process. In contrast to my experience in the American business environment, where litigation seems to be a way of life, there are few overt contractual disputes between any two reputable firms in Japan. Such exposure would be considered detrimental to the various stakeholders: customers, employees, and others who are tightly coupled to the firm. Disputes that do arise are more often resolved by *hanashiai* ("mutual discussion" or "negotiation"), in which *itamiwake* ("sharing of pain") is often used as a guideline.

Another phrase that has caught on in Japan is *kyoso to kyocho* ("competition and cooperation"), which describes a common mode of business behavior. In the United States, although there are some competitive partnerships, business executives tend to build esprit de corps around companies, partnerships, and consortia of companies as though they were fighting a war or playing a football game. They denounce competitors in public and put down competitive products by name in comparative advertising. In Japan astute foreign businesspeople realize that Japanese firms and individuals rarely take sides—and for a reason. Industry concentration tends to be high in Japan: a few major participants often account for the majority of the output. Moreover, these dominant firms are vertically integrated. To a participant in such an industry, another firm could be at once a competitor, partner, and customer, in different divisions of the company. As in the United States, not all these relationships are publicly known. Thus, taking sides—and especially burning bridges—could be disastrous in Japan.

Competition thus means different things in the United States and in Japan. U.S. antitrust laws prohibit activities that restrict competition, and competition tries to approach the laissez-faire ideal. In Japan the structure of competition is much more complex. Looser enforcement of antitrust laws allows for various shades of gray in pricing and market segmentation; experienced foreign businesspeople often say, "If this were the States, they'd be in handcuffs." As the structural impediment talks progress, many such incidents are appearing in the press. One had to do with collusion *(dango)* prior to bidding on the landfill part of the Kansai Airport Construction Project. Thus, one of the items agreed upon in the structural impediment talks calls for stricter enforcement of antitrust laws. But the Japanese government believes in keeping order in the marketplace and avoiding "market chaos and confusion." For example, MITI might provide *shidoh* in a declining industry in which capacity and supply must be wound down.

One manifestation of *kyoso to kyocho* is in the subcontracting arrangements sometimes made between competing firms. For several reasons, including the higher overhead in distribution channels, manufacturers in Japan are constantly trying to reduce costs. To achieve economies of scale and efficiency, competing firms with complementary product lines subcontract production to each other. For example, most electronics firms in Japan carry a broad product line, covering consumer to industrial goods. A firm strong in communications might ask a competitor strong in consumer products to produce its television set in return for producing the competitor's fax machines.

Another interesting aspect of competition in Japan is the concept of *yokonarabi,* which comes close to the American expression "herd instinct." It reflects the catch-up mentality mentioned earlier in the chapter. When one company introduces a successful new product, all the other firms in the industry follow suit. For example, Asahi introduced dry beer, and soon every brewer in Japan was producing an analogous product. When Toshiba produced its successful Rupo series of portable word processors, other electronics manufacturers brought out their own models, and prices declined dramatically. Often all firms pursue the same market segment; only a few notable exceptions carve out their own market niches. Often the consequence is excess capacity, leading to severe price erosion. A recent compilation of the VCR models currently being sold in Japan listed 143 models offered by 14 manufacturers, although many of these models were manufactured by OEMs (original equipment manufacturers) or subcontractors.

Thus, competition within most industries in Japan is intense. Many competitors jockey for position not only in the same product line but also in the same market segment. At the same time, the multifaceted cooperation between Japanese firms sometimes puts an upper limit on how publicly confrontational one Japanese firm can be to another, particularly if the firms involved operate according to Japanese business standards. To understand how this happens, it is useful to look at a few cases of Japanese firms in conflict.

The first case has been described by James C. Abegglen and George Stalk, Jr., in *Kaisha* (1985). In 1981, Yamaha announced its intention to displace Honda as Japan's leading producer of motorcycles, and set up a new, high-capacity plant to produce them. Honda countered with product proliferation and shortened product cycles, ultimately making Yamaha's newly established manufacturing capability obsolete. This competitive battle, which took place over a number of years, ended with a public statement of surrender by Yamaha. The whole episode was widely publicized, and some of the Yamaha people were more outspoken than Japanese culture usually allows. Such a statement rarely appears in the Japanese press.

Another example involved NEC, which held the dominant market share in the Japanese personal computer industry. Part of the reason for NEC's strength was that its rivals had refused to adopt its software and interface standards and thereby tap into the huge software base that exists for NEC. Seiko Epson decided to take on NEC by developing a personal computer that runs software written for the NEC personal computer. Seiko Epson thus became the first firm to enter the NEC-compatible market.

NEC took the unusual step of going to court. It claimed that Seiko Epson was violating NEC's intellectual property by developing a personal computer compatible with NEC's and asked for a court order halting Seiko Epson's shipments. The case attracted considerable attention because at the same time Intel, the American semiconductor firm, and NEC were contesting in U.S. courts over whether NEC had violated Intel's intellectual property rights in developing the V-series microprocessor. Those who were expecting to be able to compare the legal positions on the two sides of the Pacific were disappointed, however, because NEC and Seiko Epson decided to settle out of court, with the result that Seiko Epson was able to ship its product to the market. Both parties saw the limits of their arguments and the potential damage of an extended legal battle. Here the tradeoff was between intense competition and concern for the damaging consequences of public conflict in the Japanese business environment.

Given the delicate task of both conforming to the Japanese code of relationships and "competing and cooperating" appropriately, a foreign firm needs a long period of indoctrination to avoid acting awkwardly. A case can be made, however, that the foreign firm should not try to conform to the Japanese norms; even if it could do so, it would be almost impossible to make U.S. headquarters policy consistent with them. Total conformity is not a necessary condition to success in the Japanese market, but an understanding of these factors and an effort to move in their direction will go a long way toward developing one's business.

The Connections among Suppliers, Distributors, and Customers

The couplings on the marketing end of a firm's operation are tighter in Japan than in the United States. One form of customer relationship is probably unique to Japan—the *otokuisan,* or long-time important customer.

A number of centuries ago, firm A got an introduction from firm B to a warrior-class prospect that at the time was considered impossible to penetrate. Firm B had to guarantee all the promises and commitments of firm A. Over time, firm A was able to penetrate that difficult target. Since then, in gratitude for that introduction, firm A has purchased only from firm B those products that firm B produces; it would not consider buying from a competitor of firm B. This practice is called *shimei* or *tokumei.*

As a result, Firm A has been totally dependent on firm B for certain products for so long that firm B has had a monopoly over firm A. The economics of total dependency is an interesting aspect of the tightly coupled Japanese supplier-customer relationship. In the West, the common wisdom is that such an arrangement would disadvantage the customer (firm A) in terms of purchasing power. What could firm A do in the short term if firm B tried to set prices unreasonably high? Firm A argues that it knows the market prices, and that firm B would not break trust by trying to force up its prices. This argument goes against free-market thinking, which is supposed to result in efficiency for both the producer and the customer; but one must assume that if the arrangement has lasted for several centuries, it must work to the reasonable satisfaction of both parties.

The bond between a supplier and an important customer is strong indeed. It is personalized: commitments are rooted in specific people. In the West, the relationship between supplier and customer often involves multiple relationships: the salesperson deals with the purchasing department, quality engineers deal with evaluation engineers, and so on. Sometimes all these interactions occur ad lib, and there is no focal point of responsibility. Each person has a different decision authority; and wherever possible, problems are passed on to someone else. A course in time management I once took in the United States, in fact, advocated that strategy as a time-saving measure. In the Japanese environment, by contrast, the salesperson is usually the focal point of the sale and must attend to most problems personally. For the customer, one person together with his or her management represents the supplier firm and is held responsible for everything that relates to the sale. This tight coupling in turn forces tight coupling within the supplier's organization.

In a similar way, the manufacturer-distributor relationship is more tightly coupled in Japan than in the United States. In the United States, manufacturers and distributors are often sovereign firms on equal ground who happen to be working together to market a particular product line. The American antitrust laws serve as a check and balance to preserve this equality. In fact, distributors position themselves so that they maintain their purchasing power with respect to their suppliers.

In Japan, the relationship between the manufacturer and its major distributors is a hierarchical one that favors the manufacturer. It is difficult for a Japanese distributor to switch product lines and suppliers—a fact that in itself makes distribution outlets much more tightly coupled with manufacturers. In the United States, distributors are fairly flexible about switching or adding suppliers if it means good business; but in Japan, except for the totally independent distributor, adding or switching product lines requires the agreement of the current suppliers.

Contrary to popular belief, the manufacturer does not always have a significant ownership position in the distributor, but dependency may be established in several other ways. A manufacturer may supply close to 100 percent of the products in a particular product line, or the manufacturer may have parachuted one of its senior managers into the distributor's executive team. Financial arrangements may offer attractive payment terms. For example, whereas in the United States distributors are expected to pay suppliers within 30 days, in Japan payment terms may range up to 180 days. In effect, the manufacturer is then financing the distributor's inventory for nearly six months. The rebate structure and merchandise return policies in Japanese distribution suggest another sort of dependency. The sales process also may require a division of labor between distributor and manufacturer; for example, technical support from the manufacturer may be required. If capital equipment is needed, there may be either a subsidy or a sharing scheme. In any of these cases, there is heavy dependency between the manufacturer and the distributor, somewhat akin to the total dependency of supplier and customer described earlier.

Looking beyond the distributor to the distributor-customer relationship, we again see some differences that illustrate tight coupling. In the United States, it is possible for two distributors representing the same manufacturer to compete for the same business with a customer. In fact, antitrust laws encourage this type of competition, often called channel conflict, by prohibiting market segmentation and manufacturer control over resale pricing. In Japan, such competition is called *batting* (a term imported from English). When it occurs, the manufacturer provides *shidoh* to one of the distributors to pull back. On the surface, this practice is not permitted under Japanese antitrust laws, but it is common knowledge that business in Japan operates in this way. Of course, a distributor for a competing manufacturer can fight for the business. The customer then usually gets a good price and can enjoy a long-term, stable relationship with a distributor with respect to a set of products from a particular supplier.

BECOMING A SEMI-INSIDER

Clearly, some of these Japanese competitive parameters make it difficult for relative newcomers to penetrate the Japanese marketing scene. Some Japanese experts are even welcoming the U.S.-Japan structural impediment talks as a way to adjust potential inefficiencies caused by this mode of competition in favor of the Japanese customer at large. While these structural factors are by definition deeply rooted and hard to change, even slow progress would imply better competitive conditions for the foreign firm operating in Japan. The more such changes occur in Japan, the more important it becomes for the foreign firm to perform well in the areas of QCDS. At the same time, a foreign firm striving to become a total insider should understand the costs and tradeoffs that accompany such a status.

Being an insider in Japanese business requires having extensive financial resources, a deep understanding of Japanese relationships, human resources that can live up to those relationships, and a commitment to conform to the unwritten code of Japanese behavior. Some obvious examples of full insiders include the Mitsubishi Group affiliates such as Mitsubishi Bank, Mitsubishi Corporation, Mitsubishi Heavy Industries, and Mitsubishi Electric; Sumitomo Group affiliates such as Sumitomo Bank, Sumitomo Corporation, Sumitomo Metal, and NEC; and Japan's largest steel manufacturer, Nippon Steel Corporation.

Some would argue that no foreign firm can ever understand Japan well enough to become a full insider. In my view, the key to success in Japan is to market a desirable product with some advantage over its competition, to improve QCDS capability with respect to that product, and to become a semi-insider. Some examples of the latter among foreign-affiliated companies include IBM Japan, Fuji Xerox, and Yamatake Honeywell, with other firms such as Kodak and Digital Equipment Corporation beginning to join the ranks.

A semi-insider firm has the following characteristics:

- It operates enough business functions in Japan to satisfy the QCDS needs of the Japanese customer—which may or may not include a local plant.
- It has some way of telling Japanese society that it is in

47

Japan to stay—perhaps with a local plant or a listing on the local stock exchange.

- It is aware of what is going on in Japanese industry and participates through the triangular relationships among government, academia, and industry described earlier or through partnering with a Japanese firm.
- It associates with enough Japanese entities to be able to secure appropriate resources, both human and financial.
- It has localized its personnel sufficiently for local sales and marketing to strike the right balance between the Japanese touch and a more open relationship that must be developed with a Japanese customer for foreign executives to understand how to solve QCDS problems.
- It is coordinated and strategic in terms of condemning Japanese business practices or involving itself in public litigation.

I recommend such semi-insider status for several reasons. On the one hand, there is a world of difference in terms of business results between being a total outsider and being a semi-insider. A total outsider cannot hire good people; secure enough credibility and trust with customers to do effective marketing; or obtain access to up-to-date industry information. On the other hand, the effort required to become a total insider is monumental compared with that required for a semi-insider; and unless one is in a business severely restricted by regulations, it is usually not worthwhile. A foreign firm cannot become a total insider simply by placing a few key Japanese managers in the local (Japanese) subsidiary and trying to act Japanese.

One can debate whether the Japanese are fair or unfair

about letting foreigners into their system. If, however, Japan is a market worth penetrating from a strategic stand-point, foreign firms need to stop arguing the point, hone their QCDS performance to the satisfaction of the Japanese customer, and become semi-insiders in the Japanese business environment.

3

Where There's a Will,
There's a Way

SOME ANALYSTS ARGUE that no trade imbalance exists between the United States and Japan if the output of both countries' overseas plants is counted. Nevertheless, the popular perception is that there is a major imbalance, and perceptions drive decisions. For example, in the electronics industry, a number of Japanese firms do well in excess of $1 billion in business annually in the United States: these include Matsushita, Sony, Sharp, NEC, Toshiba, Sanyo, Canon, and Mitsubishi. By contrast, only three American firms do significantly more than $1 billion a year in business in Japan: IBM Japan, Fuji Xerox, and Nihon Unisys. Other established U.S. firms such as TI, Hewlett Packard, NCR, Honeywell, 3M, and Digital Equipment are not yet at that point. When the figures are added up, the result is a significant trade surplus in the electronics industry in favor of the Japanese. It looks as though the Japanese are winning in the United States, and the Americans are struggling in Japan.

A recent study commissioned from Booz, Allen, and Hamilton by the U.S. Chamber of Commerce shows that direct U.S. investment in Japan is much lower than Japanese investment in the United States. To understand why this might be so, one must look at the motivations for pursuing cross-cultural business.

The reason Japanese businesses originally embarked for the U.S. market is clear. During the 1950s and 1960s, per-capita income in Japan was low, and the domestic market was therefore inadequate to provide the growth to which the Japanese aspired. To become industrially competitive, Japanese business had to penetrate the U.S. market. Amid much debate on how to proceed, this goal remained clear.

By contrast, Americans today view Japan not only as a market but also as the home ground of its global competitors, as a technological and application trendsetter, as a partner, and so on. Marketing in Japan would require strategic investment in that marketplace; but in the short term, a dollar spent in a market outside Japan often yields more than a dollar spent in Japan. Many people have shown that direct foreign investment in Japan has produced long-term returns as good as or better than investments based in the United States, but the U.S. financial markets expect American corporations to provide a quick return.

Other considerations may also affect commitment to the Japanese market. Often there are tradeoffs between a thrust into the Japanese market and global strategy. Special treatment of the Japanese market may lower economies of scale, or an opportunity in another part of the world may have to be passed up. Perceptive businesspeople recognize, however, that in global industries where Japanese competition is substantial and fierce, penetrating the Japanese market in that segment is tantamount to being globally competitive. If a Japanese competitor is generating the major portion of its profit margin from the Japanese market, then aggressive pricing by the American competitor can limit the Japanese firm's war chest. Moreover, honing one's operational capabilities with respect to QCDS by addressing the same Japanese customers who drive the Japanese competitor's effectiveness can also enhance one's global competitiveness.

THE IMPORTANCE OF CORPORATE COMMITMENT

Corporate commitment is crucial to doing business successfully in Japan. Operating in a distant culture inevitably requires dealing with exceptions to standard operating procedure. If a Japanese subsidiary has to fight headquarters over every piece of bureaucratic red tape, progress will never be made.

Some American chief executives are personally committed to the Japanese marketplace. Texas Instruments' singlemindedness in entering the Japanese semiconductor market despite foreign investment restrictions, through its use of technology licenses and temporary partnership with Sony, was possible only because of the commitment of its CEO at the time, Pat Haggerty. More recently, American Express has been investing heavily in advertising for the Japanese market. Kodak has relocated Al Sieg, formerly a corporate strategist, to Japan and is carrying out an aggressive plan of acquisition, research and development, and marketing.

In my experience, however, American CEOs are rarely committed to Japan from day one. Even in the most successful American firms operating in Japan, initial interest has been coupled with skepticism, and CEO confidence and commitment have grown to total support only slowly and incrementally. Instead of, "I want to get into Japan and I've set aside X dollars to do it—tell me how," the attitude of many CEOs is, "Bring me a proposal that feels good, and I'll approve it." The proposal hardly ever feels good because of the large cultural differences, and the response is to start small. Some argue that without total commitment one should not try to do business in Japan, but not every CEO is oriented toward total commitment, and often little can be done about changing these attitudes in the short run.

The Booz, Allen study cites two reasons foreigners hesitate to invest in Japan. The first is the longer time it takes such an investment to reach average corporate profit levels, in comparison with investments outside Japan. Even Unilever, an effective competitor in consumer goods, is not satisfied with the rate of growth of its Japanese business after twenty years. The second reason is the difficulty and complexity of doing business in Japan (the problems discussed in chapters 1 and 2). By contrast, the Japanese Chamber of Commerce in New York commissioned a study done by Arthur Young that found over half the Japanese firms sampled who invested in the United States were receiving returns at least as high as expected.

THE CROSS-CULTURAL CHALLENGES

Is it, then, more difficult for Americans to do business in Japan than for Japanese to do business in the United States?

Certainly the Japanese successfully penetrated the American marketplace only after expending considerable effort and solving many complex problems. Americans have encountered similar problems in their efforts to penetrate the Japanese market. Some problems, such as tailoring a product to fit local market needs, are equally difficult for both Americans and Japanese; I call this a symmetric challenge. Other problems are asymmetric. For example, it is easier for the Japanese to hire experienced American executives to work in their U.S.-based subsidiaries than it is for American firms to hire experienced Japanese to work in the Americans' Japanese subsidiaries. Distinguishing between these symmetric and asymmetric problems is crucial to understanding where the real problems are.

The goal of this discussion is not to be negative or pessimistic about entering the Japanese market. I have, however, observed too many Americans who, having an overly optimistic view of the advantages of doing business in Japan, become discouraged. It is far wiser, I believe, to set one's expectations at the right level and to be prepared for the problems. Realism, and not false hope, is what will truly enhance one's chances of success.

Entrepreneurship in the United States and Japan

Starting up a business—specifically, the small- to medium-scale business, with which overseas subsidiaries tend to begin, in both Japan and America—is a key asymmetric challenge. Although it is difficult to start a business anywhere in the world, the difficulty is relatively greater in

Japan. In the United States a place like Silicon Valley, in California, functions as a haven for entrepreneurs. The ready availability of many essentials makes rapid start-up possible. Experienced people can be hired through head-hunters; design, manufacturing, and marketing capabilities can be obtained either as a service or as a unit through mergers and acquisitions. Do-it-yourself start-up kits are even available in bookstores, containing form letters, form contracts, and other useful material. Silicon Valley is an environment where venturesomeness is valued more than conservatism and loose coupling runs rampant. It is admittedly a special type of environment, but in a way it typifies the American business society.

Japan presents a different kind of business environment to entrepreneurs. The whole society operates, as we have seen, on *anshinkan,* and newcomers, even those with considerable technology or know-how, are not trusted. To get started in Japan, a new firm needs *hosho,* or the "backing of many people." Without *hosho* it cannot secure financing (there is no such thing as legitimate unsecured financing in Japan), hire people who prefer *anshinkan,* or attract customers. Few entrepreneurships in Japan become overnight successes in the Japanese marketplace; even the infamous Recruit conglomerate, which started in the 1950s, had to use illegal means of influencing people in power to grow as rapidly as it did before the law caught up with it.

Part of the problem is that Japan is not a do-it-yourself society. One aspect of tight coupling encountered by any entrepreneur in Japan is the need to engage multiple parties in order to transact business. The concepts of *kamaseru* ("let others share in the fruit") and *itamiwake* ("share the pain") are crucial. This tight coupling also gives rise to a society that is conservative about parceling out and selling off whole organizations and capabilities as a package.

Thus, if it is harder for the Japanese entrepreneur to set up shop in Japan than it is for the American to do so in the United States, it is then—given the enormous cultural gap—much harder for Americans to start up a business in Japan than for Japanese to do so in the United States. Nevertheless, the Japanese did encounter difficulties in entering the U.S. marketplace. Some began at a time when "Made in Japan" was construed to mean shoddy quality. Others tried to travel to the United States when the Japanese government severely restricted their ability to bring foreign exchange overseas. Many in the older generation have horror stories about trying to communicate in the United States without a knowledge of the English language. Yet by its political ideology, the United States is more open to foreigners than perhaps any other country in the world.

Challenges in the Japanese Sales Environment

Selling is hard in any environment. However, Japanese business practices render American selling concepts untranslatable as is. Having had the privilege of engaging in the industrial sales process of these two countries in the native context, both linguistically and culturally, I have first-hand knowledge of some of the differences.

Starting up a business relationship feels much harder in Japan than elsewhere. First, the superior position of the Japanese customer relative to the supplier, described in chapter 1, often conditions the purchasing manager to put up a front and yield at most a minimal amount of information about his situation. At this stage, Japanese customers are almost always unwilling to provide a supplier with an opportunity to simply "interview" the prospect.

As the customer wonders whether to engage in discussions with a new supplier, considerable emphasis is placed on factors an American businessperson might find trivial, such as posture, proper use of honorific Japanese, the way in which the business card was given, and even the way in which the sales appointment was made. A large dose of personal effort is required at the start: such persistence is a test of character. Neither product leverage nor logical sales persuasion skills means much at this stage.

One nearly always reaches the point of almost giving up in a Japanese sales situation earlier than one would in an analogous American context. Often the Japanese customer will encourage this by implying *no.* Persisting past this initial *no,* even if one has exhausted all sales logic, tends to be the key to success in Japan. One often finds that the stronger the front initially put up by a Japanese purchasing manager, the more he later "flip-flops" and becomes reasonable. More difficult is the silent but calculating person who does not let his guard down.

Even when one tries to get ahead through an introduction by a close acquaintance, things tend to work differently in Japan. There, the friend not only matches up the two parties but is also considered responsible for what happens later. If a commitment is broken, the person in the middle will be put under pressure. In addition, the party who was introduced is considered to have signed up to a commitment with the acquaintance who introduced him or her. And the salesperson will owe the acquaintance a favor, usually in a tangible form. Analogously, reference selling, in which a supplier who has a partial product line recommends another manufacturer who has the missing piece, does not work in Japan unless the recommending supplier is willing to guarantee the performance of the supplier being recommended.

Japanese customers are often more concerned about the continuity of product lines than are their American counterparts. But American firms usually have to think hard before providing information on future products and technologies to their large, vertically integrated Japanese customers, who may have a sister division that is in turn a competitor. In this situation, I usually do as the Japanese do: that is, I structure information like an "onion," providing the customer with an overview (the first layer) and, if necessary, one more layer after that. If one is properly disciplined about structuring information, one can minimize leakage of sensitive data.

Often the Japanese customer will ask for something special, such as a customized product or extra service. It is natural in the American context to ask what the return will be for that extra work. The Japanese often claim that a supplier must do that special work just to get to the "starting line"; otherwise, it cannot even be considered. In the arena of custom-integrated circuits, suppliers used to charge the customer for the engineering required to design the chips. When the Japanese jumped into the business, the value of that engineering job immediately went to zero.

To close the order, logic by itself rarely works. What does is multilevel selling of *anshinkan* with respect to the supplier. While multilevel selling is important anywhere in the world, higher management buy-in hedges against risk for working-level people; without it, they would abandon logical arguments altogether. Conversely, a top-level management meeting produces an environment where working-level people would be open to persuasion by a salesperson.

Ambiguous feedback can also present a difficulty in Japan. The absence of a Japanese equivalent for a clear *yes* or *no* is well known. Instead, the Japanese usually proceed according to the expression *ichi o yueba jyu o shiru,* meaning "know ten from hearing one." One is expected to have studied enough to understand a response from contextual information, rather than needing to ask directly.

The Japanese rarely imply a commitment to purchase, partly because they know that doing so obligates them and partly because it is not a customary practice in their culture to do so. The Japanese concept of *shugyo* ("apprenticeship") is involved here. Whatever the area—the martial arts, making sushi, Buddhism, or sales—a Japanese must spend many years, usually at least a decade, in apprenticeship before receiving any positive feedback from a teacher. Instead, the value system mandates that the individual find the proper path for himself or herself.

It is illuminating to look at the creed of a shogun whom the Japanese intensely admire—Tokugawa Ieyasu:

Man's life is like making a long journey with a heavy burden. One must not hurry.
If you regard discomfort as a normal condition, you are not likely to be troubled by want.
When ambition arises in your mind, consider the days of adversity.

Patience is the foundation of security and long life; consider anger as an enemy.
He who only knows victory and does not know defeat will fare badly.
Blame yourself, do not blame others.
The insufficient is better than the superfluous.

Not very positive in the American sense, are they? Further explanation can shed some light on these statements.

The fact that Taichi Sakaiya is not known to many educated Americans is ample evidence of the huge gaps in Japan-U.S. communications. The man is presently a best-selling social critic in Japan. He communicates clearly and is sincere about the shortcomings of Japan. In a society where anyone criticizing Japan is banished as an ignorant Japan-basher, the Japanese find Sakaiya hard to ignore. There are a couple of reasons for this. For one thing, Sakaiya is a graduate of Tokyo University and was a career bureaucrat in MITI, associated with such successful projects as Expo '70 in Osaka. Moreover, he is well-versed in Japanese history, having written a number of works on the subject.

Sakaiya explains how the Japanese have more recently extended the tradition of perseverance represented by Tokugawa Ieyasu's creed. He claims that around 1941, Japan embarked on an industrialization program that formed the infrastructure of mass production which led to the dramatic growth of the Japanese economy. This program was based on three types of standardization. The first was standardization of products: the bureaucracy categorized products and limited the types of each that could be manufactured. For example, while there were more than sixty types of rice before this time, only two grades of rice survived. The second was standardization of information. Tokyo was to set the standard for all information, homogenizing it so that consumers all over the island would react in a similar manner to advertising and other marketing information.

Perhaps the most important type of standardization was people-related. Sakaiya claims that the Japanese educational system was derived from the Nazi *folkschule* concept, which had the goal of creating people who were willing to perform chores they hated. At the elementary level, national and public schools were preferred to private schools. And students could attend only the designated school in their neighborhood. This policy accomplished two things: it controlled the educational content and standardized the profile of the student body at each school. From this approach came the tendency for the educational system to concentrate more on shoring up a student's weakness than on extending a student's strength. Thus, the average Japanese person may be educated to be exceedingly tolerant about performing tasks that are not naturally desirable. This also explains, in part, why Japanese textbooks are hard to read in comparison with their American counterparts. In America, textbooks don't sell unless they are easy to understand. In Japan, textbooks that are too easy to read are treated with skepticism. Learning is not meant to be fun in Japan—whereas in the American culture people try to minimize what they don't feel like doing.

This explanation is of interest mainly to newcomers trying to establish a relationship with a sales prospect. I have experienced both this kind of situation and one in which there was more history to the relationship. Things do get easier with time, and the profits do accrue eventually.

Some Attitudinal Challenges

In addition to the challenges offered by the Japanese business environment, American firms need to face attitudes and motives of their own that interfere with successful dealing in Japan. For example, when one is successful in an endeavor, pride in the accomplishment makes adaptation difficult. If an American firm has established a successful business system for its domestic market, that success often leads to the illusion that the formula will work universally. Kenichi Ohmae, the author of several books on Japan, has pointed to cases in which the market-share positions of two American firms in the same industry were reversed when the companies competed in the Japanese market. For example, Gillette has a much larger market share in the United States than Schick, yet Schick is doing much better in Japan. The same is true of Revlon and Max Factor. Success tends to breed inertia and inflexibility.

The American emphasis on short-term return does not help to overcome these attitudes. When one examines payback, return on investment, or internal rate of return in the short term, a realistic business plan for the Japanese market may look poor. If it looks good in the short term, one should check to see if the revenue forecast is too optimistic or the investment and expenses are projected too low. Too many American businesses take the attitude that participation in the Japanese market would simply mean more revenue leveraged from the same resource— an incremental perspective. Often this attitude leads to superficial dabbling in Japan, followed by a rude awakening and eventual pullout. The goal that will result in making the proper level of investment in Japan is long-term return combined with strategic positioning of one sort or another.

The Inherent Schizophrenia in Japanese-American Business Dealings

Working between two very different cultures can lead to a kind of schizophrenia. Japanese customers and partners tell U.S. firms to conform: "When in Rome, do as the Romans do." The result is often slow progress and impatience back at headquarters. A high-handed approach, on the other hand, has been known to produce results. Commodore Perry, after all, succeeded in opening Japan to Western trade not by trying to understand Japan but by gunboat diplomacy.

Today a more careful balance between conforming and high-handedness is crucial to success in Japan. The Japanese subsidiary of an American firm must try to satisfy two masters with divergent values and attitudes. If customers are dissatisfied, revenue goes down. If the parent company is dissatisfied, investment and product supply may go down. Every successful foreign subsidiary I have seen in Japan uses the two styles, skillfully balancing the agendas of the two important stakeholders. Using the "macho" approach too frequently usually backfires in the Japanese environment—remember, Perry didn't stay long in Japan. It may be good for one or two deals, but eventually, when there is a change in the environment, the balance of power may be reversed. Thus, basic marketing is still valid in Japan, with a little of the macho approach mixed in to stimulate otherwise conservative and inert Japanese organizations.

IT CAN BE DONE

Despite all these problems, some foreign subsidiaries have succeeded in Japan. IBM Japan has a respectable market-share position in Japan, earns higher-than-average profits from the Japanese marketplace, and contributes significantly to the worldwide strategies of the IBM Corporation. The Japanese business periodical *Diamond* annually lists the top foreign earners in Japan, and clearly a number of firms are doing an excellent job. Many of these firms, however, improved their Japanese positions despite the incremental commitment of the parent corporation. It is usually much more difficult for a subsidiary to influence its parent than it is for the parent to influence the subsidiary. Yet over the years each of these firms has made major accomplishments that motivated the parent corporation to increase its level of commitment and support.

The Phases of Penetration and Commitment

An American firm's participation in and commitment to the Japanese business environment usually develops in three phases. The first phase involves entry and initial marketing. In most cases, the American firm brings a differentiated product or service to Japan. Although some claim that differentiation is not essential, my experience is that innovation in product or service helps a foreign firm to break into the tight coupling and make up for the initial lack of marketing *anshinkan*. A unique and attractive product tends to entice potential customers who are adventurous enough to risk some inconvenience.

During this initial phase, a number of tasks must be performed well: hiring a core set of people, including the representative director of the Japanese subsidiary; establishing a distribution channel for the products; and establishing a base from which QCDS improvement can occur, especially a minimal support capability for service. Supply of product should be provided with as little interruption as possible. If an innovative product is combined with reasonable execution of these tasks, the subsidiary's sales should rise a certain amount and then level off.

The second phase—competitor catch-up—is where many Western firms fall down. As the foreign firm establishes a new product or service concept in Japan and its sales start to grow, Japanese competitors soon realize that this sales growth could mean good business for them as well. Because catch-up usually occurs with breathtaking speed, the foreign firm needs to anticipate such a threat.

To maintain a position in the market segment the new product or service helped create, a foreign firm must function at the same level of competitiveness the potential Japanese competitors strive for. By this time the customer base has usually grown beyond the innovative risk takers, so it is necessary to meet customer needs in a way that addresses *anshinkan*. That may mean changing the product or service from a standard offered worldwide to one more specifically tailored to Japanese users. At the least, it means paying attention to the QCDS expectations described in chapter 1. Living up to those expectations goes a long way toward expanding one's business and holding the line against encroaching competition. Since this expansion cannot be supported with only the core set of people organized during the first phase, stable hiring must begin, perhaps by tapping the pool of new college graduates.

When feedback from Japanese customers makes clear that one's QCDS capability is adequate, one can further penetrate the Japanese business environment by striving for the final phase—namely, becoming a semi-insider. A description of the concept of the semi-insider was given in chapter 2; and in chapters 5 and 7, I deal with some means of achieving semi-insider status, specifically in the arenas of human resource policy and partnering. A few success stories will illustrate the various routes followed.

After spending fifty years in Japan and developing a distinctly Japanese human resource and customer service policy, IBM Japan is a good example of a semi-insider, although its competitor Fujitsu still calls it an outsider. (The strong tendency in Japan is not to call any foreign entity an insider.) IBM's Japanese operations began as a maintenance outlet and sales subsidiary. Later, when Fujitsu and Hitachi started on the catch-up trail in the area of mainframe computers, IBM Japan added research laboratories and factories. In the early 1980s, NEC, Fujitsu, and several other firms entered the personal computer business; and IBM allowed an independent business unit to be formed to produce a Japanese version of the IBM

67

personal computer—the model 5550, which it farmed out to Matsushita to manufacture, and became moderately successful. During this period, IBM sales in Japan grew at an enormous rate, justifying its incremental investment.

YHP, Hewlett Packard's presence in Japan, followed a somewhat different route to semi-insidership as a joint venture with Yokogawa Electric of Japan. It is now 75-percent owned by YHP with 3,400 employees. Kenzo Sasaoka, YHP's president, describes its history in three phases: as a colony of the HP empire, as an independent nation, and as a state within the federal republic of Hewlett Packard. In the first phase, YHP had little credibility within Hewlett Packard; their business results and indicators were not impressive. In the second phase, YHP adopted the concept of total quality control (TQC), which led them on a path of fairly rapid continual improvement of their operations. (They won the coveted Deming Prize in 1982.) This step did much to gain credibility for YHP within Hewlett Packard, and it is now in the third phase where HP asks YHP for advice on certain operational decisions.

Fuji Xerox also had to develop such credibility gradually. Set up as a joint venture between Fuji Film of Japan and Rank Xerox, Xerox's British subsidiary, it operated for a while as a sales subsidiary, performing slight modifications of overseas products for the Japanese market. Producing the right product became even more important as Canon and Ricoh started the catch-up game. Later Fuji Xerox added operational capability, and its credibility picked up significantly when it originated a low-end copier that became successful in non-Japanese markets.

Sustaining Corporate Commitment

In order to maintain their success, foreign subsidiaries must maintain the interest of both their customers and their parent corporations in the face of the cultural gap. Often a foreign subsidiary in Japan will concentrate so heavily on the customers that the parent corporation loses interest and "pulls the plug." Successful subsidiaries have found that several strategies are important to sustaining the parents' interest:

- Providing business results that approach worldwide standards. Different companies use different indicators for the health of a business; but if a Japanese subsidiary is showing good indicators in profitability, market share, or productivity, or in an appropriate combination of these, most reasonable parents will keep up the support.
- Executing major strategic projects well. Such projects could include a major marketing campaign or a smooth transition when a new function requires a substantial investment such as an R&D center or a local plant. Many foreign firms have had such serious problems in putting up a plant in Japan that the parent company has resisted investment in Japan for a long time after. YHP's successful execution of the TQC program is an example of a project that gained the firm credibility.
- Becoming an integral part of the parent's global strategies. Xerox Corporation's respect for Fuji Xerox went up dramatically when a low-end copier that Fuji Xerox developed primarily for the Japanese market started to do well in the U.S. market, right in the parent's backyard.
- Keeping the parent involved. Joint strategy sessions, vis-

its by the parent corporation's senior management to key Japanese customers, personnel rotation between parent and subsidiary, and cross-cultural training all help both ends agree on responsibilities, information, and values. Such strategies are particularly important in American firms that tend to have high turnover in the senior management ranks. Maintaining relationships with multiple senior executives is crucial so that when a reassignment occurs, one does not have to go back to square one.

Key Factors in Getting Started

Getting started on the right foot requires that several basic needs be met. First, one needs a good local general manager, along with an atmosphere of trust between that general manager and the headquarters CEO/management team. The position should not be a purgatory for managers with below-par performance. I was once surprised when an American executive, talking of a colleague stationed in Japan, pointed to a map and said, "You see how close that place [Japan] is to Siberia?" Such an attitude guarantees that the CEO of the parent firm will not trust the subsidiary. Not only will the subsidiary have a hard time getting things approved, but the parent will tend to centralize and consolidate power, reducing the local decision-making authority of the subsidiary. Sometimes an American CEO even secretly hires a consultant to find out whether the subsidiary is "doing the right thing."

An American firm should have the courage to send its most talented managers to Japan, not only to contribute their skills to the efforts to penetrate the Japanese market but to continue to contribute to their firm's Japanese endeavors and global competitiveness after their return. IBM has done so with George Conrades, who some years ago headed up the Asia Pacific Group headquarters in Japan and is now climbing the ladder of high-level management. Unfortunately, an executive repatriating to the United States too often finds a minor position awaiting. A measure of the commitment Japanese firms had to entering the U.S. marketplace is demonstrated in this area. For a number of generations, the president of Mitsubishi International Corporation, the overseas subsidiary of Mitsubishi Corporation, went on to become the representative director (CEO) of its parent corporation. Akio Morita of Sony moved his family to New York, where he made numerous connections and gained experience before returning to Japan and resuming key positions in Sony headquarters.

The local general manager need not be an American; a Japanese could fill the role. I would venture to say, however, that I know few Japanese who are aggressive and persuasive enough to prevail among confrontational American executives. Often a team approach to top management of the subsidiary works. When one is operating across two distant cultures, it may be difficult to find a manager who possesses both the sales skills and the headquarters-management skills needed to do the job. In such a case, a local executive may be hired to handle the sales side and an American to deal with headquarters.

A second key factor for foreign success in Japan is segment-oriented marketing. A crucial prerequisite is market research, but many foreign firms stumble here. George Fields, in his *From Bonsai to Levi's* (1985), cites the example of the marketing of a cake mix in Japan. Because most

Japanese homes at that time did not have ovens, the firm recommended using the rice cooker. The Japanese are, however, obsessive about cooking rice so that it comes out pure white, and were therefore unwilling to use the rice cooker for making cakes.

Most American managers dislike niche-oriented strategies. They feel that such marketing does not provide enough market share. In Japan, however, companies like BMW have found that by pursuing a certain segment of the population they not only establish a stronghold, including distribution channels, but expand this market rapidly because market substitution occurs rapidly. In fact, this expansion occurred so quickly that Nissan introduced the Cima, a midrange, high-performance vehicle, to compete directly against BMW. Segment-oriented marketing combined with quick market substitution can be an effective way of expanding one's business in an environment like Japan, where breaking into an established business is practically impossible for a newcomer. After the market segment is defined, pricing, distribution, and promotional strategies consistent with that segment must be put in place.

The third key factor is maintaining continuity in marketing strategy. In the United States if firms do not see quick results, the tendency is to change something. In Japan, where stability is deemed important, such an approach has a much more negative impact than would be imaginable in the American environment. In a *Harvard Business Review* article, Theodore Levitt recounts the story of a well-known American cosmetics manufacturer's attempt to market its products in Japan. Initially the firm tried selling standard cosmetics in elite outlets. When that strategy did not produce results quickly enough, the firm placed lower-priced products into broader distribution. Again, the desired result was not obtained, and the firm changed the local president and cut back distribution. Japanese do not look favorably on such a sequence of events; it lowers the already finite probability of success. As one American executive with long experience in Japan once told me, "It takes a long time to get people back home to realize that in Japan you just can't turn things on and off like a faucet."

In a recent *Fortune* magazine article about the keys to successful business in Japan, staying power was mentioned as a major factor. Of course, in expensive and competitive Japan, long-term investment requires financial staying power. This might involve arranging to procure low-cost capital from Japanese sources to lower one's hurdle rate and to get short-term–oriented U.S. investors off one's back, at least about investments in Japan. Moreover, corporations must be willing to persist—in selling, distribution matters, negotiating with the government, and so on. The key, however, is not just CEO commitment. The whole corporation, including the Japanese subsidiary, must strive to encourage such investment by successfully executing the factors I discuss in the next chapter.

4

Responsibilities of a "Maker"

IT IS ILLUMINATING to try buying a video-cassette re-
corder in both New York and Tokyo, as I recently happened to do. Within the span of a month, I bought one
for myself in Tokyo and one in New York City for my
sister.

In Manhattan, as I walked into a consumer appliance
store, a salesperson walked up to me and took the approach
I expected—prospect qualification. He tried to help me
decide which model suited my needs. He steered me toward a model he thought was the best value for the price
range and feature set I was interested in. My simple remark, "This VCR has a G.E. brand name on it," immediately triggered a response from the salesman. "Don't
worry, it's made in Japan by Matsushita," he said. I looked
carefully at the box for the product. In fact, the firm selling
the product was CSF Thomson from France.

Since I did feel that this model could suit my needs, I
decided to compare prices at a few other stores. When I
came back after an hour or so, the salesman came at me
more aggressively, figuring that the probability of purchase

was high. He told me, "You've got five minutes to make a decision, and if it's no, so be it. I'm off in five minutes and I'm dying to see my wife, whom I haven't seen in three days." Having looked around enough, I decided to purchase this G.E. model. He looked pleased for a slight moment before he explained to me that the warranty policy was ninety days on labor, one year on parts, and pushed hard to sell me an extended warranty policy that would get me a year's worth of warranty for an extra fifty dollars. I said, "You told me it was made in Japan, didn't you?" He responded, "This is your last chance. If your VCR breaks on the ninety-first day, you're out of luck." I declined his offer. When I asked about blank tapes, he said there was a sale on tapes; these I bought and paid for separately. I hauled away the VCR and installed it in my sister's apartment.

Now let's go to Tokyo. There, I walked into an electronics retailer and found so many VCR models that I was at a loss which to pick. A salesman approached me to sort out and explain the features of the various models. He spent as much time explaining as I wished. I was simply astounded at the "adaptive creativity" of competing Japanese VCR manufacturers, all of which tried to provide better features for the user and to differentiate themselves from the competition. After choosing a model, I negotiated down from the already discounted (off-list) price. In the Japanese consumer appliance market, customers typically expect a discount of 20 percent to 25 percent off the list price. Thus, sellers often post a 10-percent to 15-percent discount off list, leaving themselves room to negotiate. I spewed out a host of arguments, bringing the price down to 25 percent off list. As I expected, the price was a little higher than what I paid for a comparable deck in New York—but the retailer delivered and installed the VCR at my house and tossed in six blank tapes for free. A couple of months later, I called the retailer regarding something I couldn't understand about the product, and the store sent someone immediately.

．　．　．

Crossing cultures, one encounters large differences in a simple transaction like purchasing a video deck. One might argue that the only difference was that I was paying for service in Japan. But I have shopped in everything from the highest-class retailers to discount stores on both sides of the Pacific, and that is not the only difference.

Also significant, for example, is the difference between what is called the American "manufacturer" and the Japanese "maker" (Japan's imported expression for "manufacturer")—a difference in concepts much more striking than the nomenclature. Let us look at the characteristics of a Japanese maker.

First is the name of the firm, the *kanban,* or—loosely translated—"brand." This is an important part of the ethos of a maker: a Japanese distribution outlet covets the privilege of being able to use the *kanban* of its supplier. Unless a firm is close to despair, it will not sell off a brand name.

Second, a maker derives significant added value from product-related endeavors, and generally not from resale margins or passive income as a rule. Thus, as mentioned in chapter 1, a maker will purchase raw materials as much as it can, and engineer the rest. Recently the proportion of operating income has gone down somewhat as a result of the rapid rise of the yen. Still, this implies that the operating managers—not financially oriented managers—make the key decisions in a firm. Investments are made to maximize competitiveness rather than asset or market valuation. In this connection, a maker is obsessed with accumulation of know-how, particularly with respect to the competition. The maker keeps up and catches up in every aspect of the evolutionary maker treadmill—product feature/performance know-how, process know-how, information management and automation know-how, manufacturing equipment and capacity investments, reducing throughput time, and so forth. Most makers as a result will buy know-how and capabilities, but are usually reluctant to sell unless it is very old technology.

Third, the maker strictly adheres to QCDS discipline, as described in chapter 1. In particular, cost reduction is a way of life, as described by the imported Japanese verb *costodaun* (the Japanese pronunciation of "cost-down"). Also, while most Japanese manufacturers officially guarantee products for one year, an aggressive customer can often ensure satisfaction for the entire useful life of the product.

Fourth, a maker tends to act like a farmer, as opposed to a hunter, regarding growth. A farmer tends to stay put in his or her territory and expand with that as a base. This is the general approach the Japanese take with respect to adding, but not terminating, major product lines; to market share orientation; to distribution organization; and so on. A hunter, by contrast, tends to move to an area with plenty of prey—thus, the profit orientation of American manufacturers and the accompanying rapid evolution toward higher-margin products, more innovative customers, and distribution channels that match product strategy.

In the Japanese market, American manufacturers must compete with the Japanese maker. In chapters 1 and 3, I examined the expectations of the Japanese customer and the importance of meeting those expectations in order to thwart competitive catch-up. In this chapter, I look at what it takes to satisfy customers in the Japanese marketplace. As in any market, the solution is simple: combine the right product with the right sales process and maintain QCDS. The challenge is to do so in a cross-cultural setting, particularly one that is culturally and physically distant.

THE RIGHT PRODUCT FOR THE MARKET

Modifying product to fit local market needs presents a symmetrical challenge: the effort required is the same, whether one is fitting an American product to the Japanese market or a Japanese product to the American market. When the Japanese first exported automobiles to the United States in the late 1950s, the cars were far from being ready for American use. Because Japanese roads were narrow and in poor condition, there was no need for a car to accelerate quickly. In the United States, however, the imports' low rate of acceleration made entering a busy freeway a difficult and risky maneuver. At normal U.S. highway speeds, the Japanese cars shook violently, and occasionally the hood flew up. Power and parking brakes were not sufficient for the hills of San Francisco, and in the harsh winters of the Northeast, the cars were hard to start in the morning. With each of these difficulties, the necessary product modification was complicated by problems in communicating the symptoms to the Japanese factory. To show the vibration of the cars, films were made and sent back to Japan. To make clear the problem of the cold start, the wife of an employee of the Japanese manufacturer took daily notes, at five o'clock in the morning, on various symptoms, such as the length of time from initial ignition to successful start. Perfecting the small vehicle did not occur overnight; when the oil crisis of the early 1970s "gave the Japanese a lucky break," they had already earned it.

Some American firms have been equally diligent in the Japanese marketplace. Johnson & Johnson made seven local product adaptations when a toothbrush that had been successful in the United States was introduced in Japan. Few firms are that persistent, however, especially when local changes require substantial engineering work. For example, an executive of a large Japanese retailer described to me his experience in importing a well-known brand of American refrigerator. The Japanese live in what they themselves call "rabbit houses," where many people occupy the equivalent of a small studio apartment. In such a home, an average-sized American refrigerator significantly reduces the living area. Moreover, the Japanese shop frequently at nearby stores and have no need for the large storage capacity required for American families who tend to buy a week's worth of groceries at a time. Perhaps even more troubling was the noise of the refrigerators. Americans rarely sleep in the same room with a refrigerator, so the noise is not particularly bothersome, but a refrigerator that sounds like an automobile engine is unacceptable in a small studio apartment.

The retailers received so many complaints that they asked the American manufacturer to consider creating a smaller, quieter refrigerator for the Japanese market. Of course, the investment in such a model for what would initially be only a small market in distant Japan promised a low return, and the proposal was rejected. The retailer had to take back all the units from the customers. By contrast, some Korean manufacturers tried in the late 1980s to penetrate the Japanese market with refrigerators more consistent with the needs of the Japanese household. Priced 30 percent lower than an analogous Japanese product, these products, which were carried by adventurous Japanese retailers, sold out season after season.

Why are some American firms reluctant to modify their products for local use? Contrary to some Japanese opinion, it is not that Americans are inept at marketing; there is another dynamic at work. As we have seen, when a foreign firm in Japan goes through phase one of marketing a new product and it is the only game in town, sales grow for a time. Innovative users put up with a product that is not tailored for Japanese needs if it is basically useful. But as phase two arrives and competitors introduce substitute products better geared to the market, maintaining market share necessitates at least matching those improvements. The Japanese subsidiary of the foreign firm then calls for a tailored product, aggressively priced. If the subsidiary does not have a development facility, it has no choice but to have development work done in the United States. This situation alone is usually enough to give the market away to the Japanese competition, because of the time needed to fight the project-priority wars. Even when the subsidiary does have a development facility, it usually has to get approval from the parent company to go ahead with the development.

I once tried to help a Japanese quality-assurance manager persuade American headquarters to configure a Japanese version of an electronic product that would be more appropriate to the operating conditions of the Japanese market. Making this change would involve two extra steps at the end of the manufacturing process. The Japanese manager, in asking for cooperation from American headquarters, mentioned that Nissan was selling automobiles with steering wheels on the left-hand side in the United States (the Japanese use right-hand-side steering wheels). The answer came back, "If you can sell as many of our products in Japan as Nissan can sell cars in the American market, I'll do it."

In addition to return on investment, other issues arise when the parent company has a worldwide product portfolio strategy, particularly if the industry is global. These issues include duplication of effort; product development in other regions cannibalizing each other in a particular marketplace; and development tradeoffs, such as deploying resources to complete a product line rather than tailoring a product for Japan. The Japanese subsidiary then must begin the long, arduous process of justification. Even getting a hearing may have to wait until the next scheduled series of strategy discussions, and many meetings may be required before American management understands the needs of the Japanese customer and their importance. Especially for a Japanese manager not fluent in English, it is an uphill battle to convince a manager in America that a remote market is going to be eaten away when that manager is hearing daily from local U.S. salespeople that they need a winner. If the original product has done well in Japan, the sentiment is likely to be, "If it ain't broke, don't fix it." Finally, the project may be approved and started, only to be canceled because of a change in the worldwide product strategy and priorities.

The effectiveness of the Japanese at the catch-up game means that any such delay should be minimized. Akio Morita, chairman of Sony, says that America is good at invention but not necessarily at innovation. According to Morita, invention is only one-third of innovation; the other two-thirds—realization of a product and marketing—are often not given enough emphasis.

When the Japanese play the catch-up game, they often attempt what they call a "plus alpha minus cost" strategy: that is, simply taking an existing product, adding features, and subtracting cost and perhaps size. This strategy has earned the Japanese the description "adaptively creative." Some examples are Canon's and Ricoh's plain paper copiers, Roland's digital pianos, and Toshiba's portable computers. In each of these products, the price of the Japanese version is lower than that of the original product and value is added. And each of these firms is actively marketing the product in the low-end category in the American market—clearly demonstrating that participating in the Japanese market and listening to the Japanese subsidiary can provide an American firm with a head start in understanding where on its own home ground the Japanese will strike next.

A significant delay in modifying a product for the Japanese market leaves the Japanese subsidiary with one of two poor choices: to watch as Japanese competition walks away with market share; or to fight to get back lost share, a choice that usually costs many times the amount of a more timely investment. But even those who do end up modifying a product usually do so only after foot shuffling in the market. Mattel's sales of its Barbie dolls suffered in Japan until it changed the appearance of the doll to straight black hair and Oriental-looking eyes. Procter & Gamble saw an improvement in detergent sales only when it realized that the Japanese use a lower water temperature in their washing machines than Americans do, and formulated a new liquid detergent for Japanese consumers. Even the now-respected BMW Japan went through a number of years of stagnant sales before it revamped its sales channels, set up a parts center capable of twenty-four-hour turnaround, introduced right-side steering wheel options in its automobiles, and reduced prices—thus eliminating many gray-market dealers who were doing parallel importing.

SELLING THROUGH DISTRIBUTION

Distribution channels are increasingly being pointed to as a nontariff barrier to trade in Japan. Certainly, they are not easy to deal with. But, again, from the standpoint of the foreign businessperson in Japan, one cannot simply complain about it; one must find a way to work with it. This is one arena where I don't feel that generalizing across industries helps much. While my informed guess is that the issues I run across in the electronics industry are similar to those grappled with by others, the manifestations are almost certain to be different.

Understanding the Differences between U.S. and Japanese Distributors

A reasonably good understanding of the role of the Japanese distributor is a prerequisite to setting up distribution channels in Japan. Thinking of the Japanese distributor as analogous to that in the United States leads to a lot of frustrations. In the semiconductor industry, for example, manufacturers use distributors in the U.S. market to cover distant territories and customers who have not reached sufficient business volumes to warrant working directly. In these accounts, distributors are often asked to do almost all of the sales support themselves. Other larger accounts and territories are taken direct. Many major Japanese manufacturers do most of their business through distribution. While these distributors play a key financial and operational role, much of the strategic selling is done with the manufacturer's direct support. Thus, whether a distributor is an integral part or an extension of one's sales capability is an important distinction.

Distributors in the United States tend to be independent. Their ability to carry competing product lines, which many distributors actually do, depends on their purchasing power. In America, diversity tends to create "peace of mind" in the distributor. In Japan, key semiconductor distributors are almost always aligned with major Japanese manufacturers. While few of them are outrightly owned by the manufacturers, they are completely dependent from a supply standpoint. They would not consider carrying a competing Japanese product line; the only products they would carry other than their principal's are those complementary to the principal's products. The supplier-distributor relationship tends to be vertical—one where on the surface the distributor must look subservient to the supplier. This "attachment" of distributors to manufacturers tends to evoke the image of a closed-channel structure in Japan, hard for foreign manufacturers to break into.

Setting Up: Picking the Right Partner or Creating Your Own Distributor

In the light of this observation about affiliations, it is not practical to try to persuade major distributors with loyalties to major Japanese competitors to carry a competing foreign product. There are, however, four other possible approaches.

The first is to target a Japanese distributor who may have loyalties but to whom the foreign product is complementary. A certain affiliated distributor in the computer arena may have a good processor product line, but may be missing peripheral products because the affiliated manufacturer doesn't handle them. The second approach is to target independent distributors. Many Japanese industries are undergoing changes in the distribution structure, with many new entrants. Manufacturers not traditionally in the electronics industry are setting up distribution outlets, Japanese trading houses are setting up electronics-related distributors, and it is amazing how quickly some of these distributors come up to speed. A third approach would be to set up one's own distributors as well, although this would require some experience in the Japanese marketplace. And finally, one could partner with a Japanese manufacturer carrying a complementary line of products and have the product distributed through the partner's sales channels.

There are two important factors to consider when setting up distributors. The first is picking the right distribution partner—obvious and easy to say, but as statistics show, hard to do. In the electronics industry, I have seen a very high incidence of the first distribution partner not working out, resulting in a very painful adjustment process. The second factor is that even if one signs up a distributor, one cannot simply expect to acquire ready-made sales capability as one might be able to in the United States. One has to work relentlessly to get the commitment and execution necessary for the distribution to be an effective sales channel for the product concerned.

The Terms of the Distribution Arrangement and Securing Commitment from Distribution Management

Top management commitment on the distributor side is obviously key to inducing the proper level of investment necessary to support and execute various sales and marketing programs. Such investment judgment can affect many areas—the assignment of human resources, the effort put into training the troops on the product line, advertising/public relations, and management's personal attention.

Needless to say, the terms and conditions under which

one signs up a distributor make a big difference. The first issue that arises is whether to grant exclusive or non-exclusive marketing rights. The former technically means that a foreign firm cannot even market through its own subsidiary; thus, a lot of leverage is forfeited. I find that American firms are more liberal in providing exclusive marketing rights in Japan than back in their home market. It would be all right if the reason were intentionally to ensure distributor commitment and start a close partnership on the right foot. Often, however, the attitude has more to do with the fact that executives in the foreign firm don't know anybody else in Japan anyway, and don't necessarily wish to be bothered by major problems in a market they consider solely incremental to their own.

When negotiated properly, exclusive arrangements do make a difference in initial commitment. I took the same product to two trading houses in Japan—one with whom I discussed an exclusive relationship, the other with whom I discussed a non-exclusive one. The former offered five times as many people and ten times as much funding as the latter. One factor that is important to watch out for, particularly when dealing exclusively with a distributor in a product that requires support know-how, is that if the principal does not invest in some local personnel of its own to provide that know-how to the distributor and becomes dependent on distributor personnel for all support in Japan, switching distributors would be difficult should things not work out.

As to financial incentives, the proper margin structure, for example, would depend heavily on the nature of the product handled and on how much work they do. In conjunction with the issue of commitment, however, it is most powerful when financial rewards complement a more basic strategic and intangible need of the distributor's, such as a prestigious brand, a much-needed complementary product line, or a product that helps in a diversification strategy. On a more tactical note, I have encountered distributors willing to take a 50-percent cut in margin because they were going to penetrate an account they considered important for another product line they carried. Also, I have seen situations where paying attention to the *kamaseru* and *itamiwake* (share in the fruit and pain) concepts (see page 56), and occasionally allowing distributors to take business that might logically be taken direct, sometimes goes a long way toward supporting commitment for other accounts.

Another challenge inherent in motivating Japanese distributors relates to that ubiquitous issue in dealing with the Japanese—feedback. While it is possible to understand the operational frustrations Japanese distributors experience from day to day, many more serious and complex problems tend not to surface. Again, few Japanese will voluntarily come forth during business hours to discuss such problems. Instead the focus shifts to after-business-hours activities. Not only is drinking a popular method for obtaining feedback, but Japanese companies frequently use overnight trips for this purpose. I remember an incident where after sales training for the distributors, a questionnaire was passed out to get feedback on its effectiveness. The results were favorable. A couple of weeks later, rumors started to surface about the inadequacy of the training. Thus, nowadays I often make it a point to take a couple of the trainees out to an informal dinner right after the training to get some frank feedback about how things went.

If affordable, training spread over two days combined with drinking late on the intervening night does a lot in this direction as well. (This may give some insight into why the Japanese have little personal time.)

Working with the Distributor

In day-to-day operations, it is easy to forget that the distributor is a separate company (often more Japanese than the foreign affiliate's Japanese subsidiary). In order to facilitate tracking of sales efforts, one must work to establish a common operating methodology, vocabulary, and set of core cultural values. I have personally found that even if a manufacturer proposes a highly structured sales review, and the distributor agrees to follow it in principle, making that system produce useful feedback for action takes at least a year or two. For example, some people in the Japanese distributor may not report lost business in sales reviews because to do so would mean a loss of face. Likewise, they may not ask for help when they need it because asking would imply lack of ability.

Even from a vocabulary standpoint, simple words such as "objectives," "sales strategy," and "return" tend to have different meanings; thus, synchronization often becomes necessary. Cultural alignment is even more difficult. Often the distributor may have a Japanese supplier in addition to a foreign one, and may be used to the Japanese supplier's way of responding to customer complaints. Simple differences can cause amazement. One distributor called a foreign manufacturer's local subsidiary, said that the customer was upset, and requested that a sales manager visit the customer. The local sales manager did the logical thing and asked what the problem was; then he delved into the issue by asking a number of questions the distributor could not answer. Thus, the sales manager asked the distributor to find out more before he would commit to a visit. The distributor expressed amazement. I heard that a Japanese supplier the distributor also deals with would not have questioned the fact that the customer was upset, and would have immediately sent someone over. That, according to his perception, was the Japanese "way."

In order to overcome these differences, it is always useful not to stop at discussion, but to act jointly. Going out to accounts together in a "buddy" fashion can uncover a lot of facts about what is really going on. Since selling a foreign product with differentiation sometimes requires a different approach than does a commodity product, a buddy call could help to teach by example. I have seen cases where the local salesperson would directly challenge the customer's premise. Though that may be the right thing to do, the distributor's representative who accompanied the local salesperson on that account visit may get extremely nervous and ask afterward, "How dare you speak like that to the customer?" It also helps to have a personnel-exchange program, in which people from either side can live in the other's environment for a temporary period in order to bridge any gaps in perception.

Perhaps the most important aspect of working with the distributor is the role the local subsidiary must play in buffering the distributor from discontinuities arising from U.S. policy changes. Termination of products and changes in licensing strategies come as real culture shocks to those distributors who carry Japanese products as well. The best solution, of course, is for American headquarters to make the transition in a smooth manner. But if it does not, the local subsidiary may have to keep support personnel and spare parts for a discontinued product in Japan longer than the U.S. policy warrants.

WINNING THE QCDS BATTLE

A foreign affiliate in Japan can attain the requisite levels of quality, cost, delivery, and service if it satisfies two requirements: an efficient factory supplies the goods, and a disciplined organization delivers goods and services to the customers. Crucial to the latter are several major issues involving centralization versus decentralization, cross-cultural interface and operating methodology, and international problem-solving skills.

Tuning the Factory to QCDS

A number of years ago, I saw a Japanese television broadcast of a college course on production management. That manufacturing was being taught on television was startling, but even more interesting was the instructor's statement that the main outputs a factory needs to control are quality, costs, delivery lead times, and production quantity—with the exception of the last, three of the four QCDS factors. (Service is not primarily controlled by the factory.) To be successful in Japan, manufacturing must have its act together.

Quality

Philip Crosby, in his *Quality Is Free* (1979), states that managing for quality is akin to a good performance of ballet; when the conductor marks a beat, the dancer steps to that beat. In a course in quality management I once took in the United States, the instructor defined *quality* as conformity to customer specifications. I asked, "I know the Japanese are very capable of conforming, but do the Americans like to conform?" The ensuing discussion made clear that they do not; the prevailing opinion seemed to be, "Hell, no, I want to do it my way." Perhaps that is why Americans are so good at playing football. It is an individualistic game: the group may decide on a certain strategy, but at the last minute the quarterback can make a judgment call that turns into a heroic maneuver.

Conformity leads to uniformity and regularity; individualism leads to irregularity. Conformity is not only demanded by Japanese management but reinforced day in and day out. Japanese factory workers wear uniforms. Watching the morning exercise is almost like watching a ballet: people try to synchronize their movements, paying particular attention to form. I once ran the same Japanese exercise program for a group of American employees in the United States: it did not occur to them to try to coordinate their movements.

The difference between Japanese and American attitudes is also apparent in the concern for defects. The Japanese attitude toward defects is uncompromising, as their famous zero defect (ZD) program suggests. The Americans criticized ZD as unrealistic, arguing that defects always occur. The Japanese agreed, but also believed in the "aim high, achieve high" philosophy. They began measuring defect levels in terms of parts per million instead of parts per hundred (percentages).

At the time the Americans were following a policy of accepted quality level, which tried to strike a balance between a tolerable defect level and the cost required to attain that level of quality. We now know that better quality actually costs less. At a lecture I attended, W. Edwards Deming, the American statistical control expert, discussed the economic merits of investing in "doing it right the first time." About half the people I talked with after the lecture said that they did not necessarily agree with Deming. In Japan, however, Deming is practically a god: people listen to what he says. In a magazine article, the auto industry expert L. P. Sullivan reports that in Japan 90 percent of engineering changes are completed six to twelve months prior to a product's introduction; while in the United States, 90 percent of engineering changes are completed three to six months after the product's introduction. This latter situation must be very costly to the manufacturer. Also, I can't see how in the latter situation the customer can obtain a good-quality product.

The uncompromising attitude of the Japanese is combined with a characteristic of Japanese culture that is expressed as *no missu*. The word *missu* is imported from English and means "miss" or "mistake." *No missu* is heard everywhere in Japanese society, from the golf course to the performance stage. In the case of manufacturing, it means "no defect." If the consensus is to do a certain operation in a certain way for maximum uniformity and an operator does not follow the guidelines, that is considered a *missu* and it becomes highly visible.

Not only do the Japanese demand cleanliness and order in the factory and refuse to accept that quality output can proceed from a dusty and cluttered environment, but the input to the manufacturing process must be good. In many Japanese factories, supplier programs have improved the quality of parts to the point where incoming inspection is no longer necessary. The supplier's design and engineering departments assure that a part is manufacturable, even down to such details as whether the slot of a screw is set vertically or horizontally on a part to be manufactured by a robot. Even so, there are numerous checkpoints and elaborate testing throughout the manufacturing process. The effectiveness of these efforts is apparent in the small size of the rework area. According to the Japanese concept of total quality control, everyone from the general manager of the plant down to the individual operator is sensitive to quality.

Cost

The Japanese attitude toward minimizing costs is astounding. The development of the Japanese economy began with the leveraging of low wages; but as time passed, that advantage became more difficult to maintain. In fact, given current exchange rates, the Japanese worker costs more than his or her American counterpart. In addition, events like the oil crisis and the twofold appreciation of the yen over a two-year period have challenged the ability of the Japanese to continue to thrive as a major industrial force. To guarantee survival and peace of mind, the Japanese proceeded to economize. American managers probably would be shocked by the measures Japanese companies take to effect savings that are sometimes measured in *sen,* a unit of currency smaller than the yen. One consumer appliance firm decided to shorten its cord specifications by a few millimeters in order to save material costs, and then told its cord supplier to reduce the price of the cord. Another firm does not allow an employee to get a new pencil until the old one, sharpened down to a length of three centimeters, is turned in. Such a measure might not be worth taking in itself, but imagine what it does to the seriousness of the attitude toward costs of employees who may be making decisions with greater economic impact. In Japan, the general feeling is that if people are wasteful, the country cannot survive.

Another aspect of minimizing costs has to do with hidden costs. Although material and direct labor costs can be seen and measured, other aspects of manufacturing—such as costs of carrying inventory, switching over equipment, and handling too many product lines—are not as visible. One Japanese firm had a program called 3Ms to eliminate *muda* ("waste"), *mura* ("irregularity"), and *muri* ("abnormal coercion"), all cost-generating factors that are hard to see. Uncovering such hidden cost items is more easily done in a tightly coupled organization with overlapping functional expertise than in a loosely coupled organization, where cost items can fall through the cracks.

A specific example of such a cost is that of bad quality. The Japanese intentionally make the costs of recovering from bad quality high to motivate firms to fix the situation causing the bad quality rather than try to get away with poor quality. For example, when a customer's computer system goes down, the manufacturer of the system sends an engineer immediately and also keeps the engineer on the scene until the problem is fixed, if necessary sending in more help and working overtime. Such an approach is costly for the manufacturer and thus underscores the need for quality products from the start. Manufacturers of export products do not initially have service centers overseas near the market, so the costly alternatives are establishing contract-repair arrangements or returning the product all the way to Japan.

In some loosely coupled American firms, some of these issues never surface. The people who run the product divisions often do not know the cost of recovering from quality problems. If these managers were forced to add up the labor, parts, and opportunity costs associated with recovery of an irate customer, and if these costs were fully charged to the division responsible for the product and to related manufacturing functions, there would be greater incentive to turn out good products. Many American firms do not understand these hidden costs because the operations that do the recovery—sales and service—are often functional organizations that are only loosely coupled to the product divisions. They are frequently revenue or cost centers; and even if they are profit centers, they operate independently of the profit and loss of the product divisions and therefore are not motivated to research and pass on information on costs. This leads to an "open loop" problem where the appropriate feedback does not transfer from the field to the factory.

In pricing, Japanese market-share mentality contrasts with American profit orientation. When a customer asks for a price that is unreasonable in relation to current product costs, an American firm often passes up the business because of the inadequate margin. Unless the request is absurd, however, a Japanese firm will follow the maxim *sonshite tokushiro,* or "take a loss first, and then take a profit." While there are some extreme examples, like Fujitsu's making a one-yen bid for a public computerization project, the more usual pattern is for the Japanese firm to take the business at a loss initially and then work on the manufacturing costs until a profit can be squeezed out of the customer relationship in the long term. This approach drives some Japanese companies to have monthly cost-reduction targets that they enforce not only on themselves but also on their suppliers and contractors.

Delivery

Meeting delivery commitments operationally requires a predictable, constant production process combined with a good factory management system. A production process may be either loose or taut. A taut production line maintains a continuous flow and a low inventory of work in progress. In such a process, problems that may be hidden in a loose production process—unbalanced production lines, badly maintained equipment, unavailability of parts—are revealed. Because goods do not spend time in work-in-process inventory and materials are kept moving on a first-in/first-out basis, output is constant and predictable. To support such a system, other capabilities are critical, including a planning system for material requirements that keeps the line operational, optimal factory scheduling and loading, regular equipment maintenance, and good supplier and labor relations. Automation is not only likely to cut costs but ensures accurate regularity in the production process.

The customer measures delivery lead time from order to shipment at the doorstep, so the production process as well as the entire order administration process must be examined. Many Japanese factories have a computerized network that spans sales offices, headquarters, the factory, distributors, and sometimes even major customers. Orders are matched with lot numbers on the production line, so that salespeople can at any time call up the status of an order on a terminal in the sales office. Such lot control also allows tracking of products through distribution channels to customers and can serve a critical role in solving quality problems.

If sales forecasts were always accurate, the capabilities just described would be enough to meet customer needs for delivery. When that is not the case, the ability to respond quickly to volatility in demand is crucial. The primary factor in handling quick increases in demand is short manufacturing lead times: that is, not only must the manufacturing process itself be short, but suppliers and subcontractors must cooperate to minimize their lead times on short notice. A long-term partnership with these vendors is therefore important. When the manufacturing capability cannot respond quickly enough to meet incremental demand, an inventory of finished goods must be maintained. And where a customer's inconvenience is at stake, it is not unknown for an employee of the distributor to hand-carry the goods from a local plant or the airport to the customer.

Service

As noted earlier, service is not generally in the domain of the factory but in that of other departments in the company. One aspect of service in which the factory can make a great deal of difference, however, is flexibility. Recently the Japanese have made great strides in the technology of flexible manufacturing. Car manufacturers can now make a wide variety of models on one production line by drastically reducing equipment set-up time and negotiating for just-in-time delivery by lots. Even semiconductors, which involve a complex production flow and hard-to-handle materials, can be automated in a flexible manner. A number of Japanese factories are making a wide variety of custom products, from gate arrays to even more sophisticated items, with a very short manufacturing lead time. Even more amazing, because of the number of package types and varying lot sizes, is the automated assembly process for such products. Eventually operational capabilities such as these will make a great deal of difference in the degree of freedom a salesperson has in making service offers to a customer.

DEVELOPING GLOBAL PROBLEM-SOLVING CAPABILITY

The factory, of course, plays an integral part in the QCDS battle. If, however, the factory is not on Japanese soil, large cultural, physical, and time-zone differences place foreign firms at a disadvantage relative to Japanese competitors with local operations. Methods of problem solving must be found that add the least possible overhead to raw factory performance. Several issues here are important, including organizational and interface design and operating methodology.

Centralization versus Decentralization

Basic to organizational design is the question of centralization. Either extreme is generally inefficient: overcentralization allows too little flexibility for overseas operations to adjust to local conditions, whereas extreme decentralization risks lack of coordination and tremendous waste. The decision is generally made from the perspective of the home office or headquarters, which is usually the power center of the corporation worldwide. To avoid bias in corporate decision making which jeopardizes one overseas operation at the expense of another, some firms have considered having multiple headquarters. One CEO of an American electronics firm decided to have his staff spend a significant amount of time in Japan, a market as big as his headquarters market. Honda has allegedly considered establishing a second worldwide headquarters in the United States, and Matsushita is thinking of executing a four-pronged headquarters strategy around the world. Much of the trade friction between Japan and the United States revolves around which country benefits in terms of financial return and employment. If American firms lose market share, that means fewer jobs and less money in the American economy. If Honda, for example, were head-quartered in Ohio with a good number of Americans on its executive staff, Americans, though still possibly anxious, would surely have less to object to.

The question of centralization versus decentralization is complex. Often excessive centralization comes from distrust of the Japanese subsidiary. Such decision making ensures that there are checks and balances in the system so as to avoid inappropriate action. In extreme cases, centralization leads to the U.S. parent's colonialization of the subsidiary, so that none of the profits earned in Japan can be automatically reinvested there. In addition, there are often two conflicting factors: local market needs and worldwide efficiency. To meet market needs, American firms usually have to go through the phases of penetrating the Japanese market that were outlined in chapter 3. An American corporation could start marketing its products in Japan by establishing a simple sales office, then adding testing capability to ensure quality products, and next adding some product modification capability to cater to special local needs. A manufacturing plant might follow. As business expanded, a more complete set of functional capabilities would need to be close by.

In terms of worldwide efficiency, one approach is to centralize resources where duplication of expensive capital-intensive facilities and operations proves wasteful. Coordination is also important. For example, having manufacturing facilities in every market one serves is clearly inefficient and makes it impossible to realize economies of scale. Fragmented product development efforts could lead to reinvention of the wheel; and other important factors enter in as well, such as trade protectionism, labor costs and availability, foreign exchange, and tax benefits and liabilities.

Usually it is best to strike a tradeoff between local market needs and worldwide efficiency. In terms of research and development, for example, the core design can be done in one location according to specifications drawn up by planners from around the world. The core design then can be transferred to the various geographic markets that have product modification capabilities. A number of central manufacturing locations can be established, with subcontracting relationships around the world to respond to local needs and swings in demand. Let us look more specifically at how a Japanese subsidiary can strike the right tradeoff between centralization and decentralization, adding value to the QCDS capability of the firm even without a major investment such as a local plant.

Quality

A completely centralized firm ships product as is from a factory not in Japan to a Japanese customer. In one case I was involved with, it was clear that the product did not meet the needs of Japanese customers. They were angry and asked for a complete analysis and plans for corrective action. Repeated quality problems swamped the local quality personnel and created poor morale. Sales personnel were not comfortable selling the product.

I immediately put in 100-percent visual outgoing inspection in Japan. Quite a few cosmetic defects were caught locally, and the defect rate was lowered significantly. I then made arrangements to put in functional testing, which caught a good portion of the remaining defects. Through these procedures, problems between the local subsidiary and the customers were converted to problems between the local subsidiary and headquarters; we removed the customers from the loop.

We tracked the improvement of quality indicators with several Japanese customers; and as they saw the dramatic results, their attitude began to change. One of our local people said, "I didn't think that customer's quality manager ever smiled. Well, he did."

When failure occurs, a completely centralized organization sends the defective product back to the United States for analysis and corrective action. We put in local quality control capability, so that for the problems that could be analyzed and fixed locally, the customer could be provided with quick turnaround. That sounds like an obvious step, but it involves negotiating, acquiring resources in the form of parts, tools, and personnel, and—ironically enough—assuring that the quality standards of headquarters will be upheld.

Pricing

In a completely centralized firm, the local subsidiary must negotiate with U.S. headquarters every price quotation below list price. That makes for a slow response, and the lack of value added of the local subsidiary soon becomes evident to the Japanese customer, who quickly loses respect for the firm.

If the parent wishes to control pricing, it can set a price floor the Japanese subsidiary is authorized to quote to. Of course, that minimum price level must be somewhat competitive; a high price floor would be tantamount to centralized operation.

If the subsidiary gets product from the parent through

a transfer pricing arrangement, it is possible to negotiate the total profit or margin the subsidiary must show and to leave the subsidiary with considerable flexibility in pricing. It can use pricing to penetrate a market with one product line and make up margin on a different product line. Or it can put together an attractive all-in-one price for a Japanese customer who wishes to do one-stop shopping by using *donburi kanjo* (discussed in chapter 1).

Delivery

A centralized firm delivers only according to the sales forecasts turned in by the subsidiary. Exceptions have to be negotiated individually.

If the variation or perishability of a set of products does not rule out the possibility of strategic inventory, much can be done. Inventory can be held in three places: at the factory, earmarked for Japan; at the local subsidiary; and at the customer site. Clearly, the farther the customer is from the factory, the more difficult it is to react to a last-minute change by the customer. Strategic inventory can provide a great deal of flexibility in delivery to the Japanese customer, but obviously one must keep a close eye on excess inventory to avoid financial risk.

With products not easily put in inventory, Japanese firms often use what are referred to as *mikomi hatchuu,* whose literal translation is "expectation orders." If the customer is likely to want something in two weeks and the lead time is four weeks, the salesperson makes a judgment call and places an order before the purchase order is received. Many American firms do not permit this type of risk taking by the sales force. If, however, a Japanese competitor has a short manufacturing lead time and a strategic inventory policy and allows *mikomi hatchuu,* Japanese customers will complain if the American firm is unable to deliver on comparable short notice. One important factor that limits the risk in this kind of expectation ordering is an accurate cultural reading of the purchaser's state of mind, which is much easier to acquire when one has an ongoing relationship with the customers.

Service

In heavily centralized operations, local personnel have no flexibility in tailoring service. For example, quite a few American firms still offer products with explanations and other internal documentation written in English. Although it is true that most Japanese customers do not understand the effort it takes to translate technical jargon, it is understandable that when a Japanese competitor provides an alternative in the local language, the customer is likely to favor that firm.

In chapter 1, I discussed what the Japanese look for in terms of service. Even if there is a limitation in capability, local personnel can make a significant difference in the way communication and problem solving are approached with the customer. That is true not only of direct subsidiary personnel but also of distributors and retailers who represent the manufacturer.

Recently I was using a Japanese hand-held computer to do simple word processing. In the process of storing the document, something went wrong and I lost a good day's worth of work. In this case, three vendors were involved: the manufacturer of the computer (a Japanese firm), the manufacturer of the word-processing software (a U.S. firm), and the distributor of the word-processing software (the U.S. branch of the Japanese firm). I called all three, explaining the situation and asking whether there was any way to retrieve the document.

A representative of the U.S. manufacturer of the software told me that, since support responsibility belonged to the distributor, he could not provide assistance. Moreover, even if he were authorized to provide it, the procedure would be so complicated that he couldn't possibly help. "You made a mistake," he added, "and it's gone."

I then called the distributor. He was a little more helpful, mainly because I told him that I was calling from Japan. He gave me some pointers, but he said that the retrieval program would be a one-day project for him and that, with the best of intentions, he couldn't help.

I finally called the Japanese computer manufacturer, whose service representative not only tried talking me through several operations over the phone, but wrote a workable program for me that retrieved the document. It is notable that, though the Japanese firm had the weakest connection to my problem and he could have referred me elsewhere, he did not.

A Japanese subsidiary staffed with the type of people exemplified by the service representative just mentioned would result in many contented customers. In order to achieve this, however, U.S. headquarters and the management team in the local subsidiary would have to value such service performance. Clearly, what that service representative did was less time-efficient than simply shrugging off the customer.

Many American firms in Japan have found creative ways

of improving QCDS without full functional decentralization. In all these cases, however, what has made such creativity possible is the cross-cultural understanding of senior management in the parent corporation.

International Organization and Interface Design

Within an international organization, the design of the international interfaces makes a significant difference in the productivity of personnel. The two most common patterns are the global product organization and international division–based organization.

The global product organization explicitly recognizes the fact that a truly global industry needs worldwide consistency in strategy, particularly in product lines. In such a design, product divisions are responsible for marketing their products worldwide, and there are as many reporting lines as there are product lines. An organization in Japan marketing a particular product line would report to the division in charge of that product line.

The international division–based organization recognizes that a firm must have a unified thrust into an important marketplace such as Japan. Typically, all the international marketing–related organizations, including overseas subsidiaries, are consolidated in such a division. Organization charts of many Japanese and American firms show this type of design. IBM Corporation has organized IBM Japan under the Asia-Pacific Group within the World Trade Corporation. Many Japanese corporations organize their overseas subsidiaries to report to a structure called *kaigai jigyo* ("overseas activity group").

In reality, however, the underlying organizational dynamics are not clear-cut. Power relationships in organizations can come not only from reporting lines but from supplying and accepting products. An overseas subsidiary that reports to the international division had better listen to the product division that it accepts products from and depends on for the bulk of its revenues. Often such relationships are shown on internal organization charts as matrix (dotted-line) relationships. The more global the industry, the stronger the relationship with the product division is likely to be.

Either organization can create a number of potential pitfalls. Trouble can result when the senior manager in the overseas subsidiary reports to a fairly high level at headquarters and there is little reporting relationship lower in the organization. If the firm is run in a highly centralized manner, the senior managers can end up spending a large portion of their time simply communicating with headquarters and solving problems below their level of detail; one senior manager in the Japanese subsidiary of an American company told me that he spends more than 80 percent of his time communicating with the United States—an untenable situation.

In matrix organizations, managers in the subsidiary report to more than one person, perhaps a local supervisor and one or more managers in the United States. Such an organizational sructure can work if it is not hampered by a lack of discipline. Often, however, dual or more reporting relationships are formed not because they are legitimately necessary but because tough issues have not been resolved. Such looseness can result in a spaghettilike tangle of needless relationships that raises the communication overhead exponentially.

Another challenge for matrix organizations involves arbitration. Because of the large cultural gap, an employee of the subsidiary may have two bosses—one in Japan and one in the United States—who differ on a particular issue. In such a case, it is crucial for the two bosses to have a good working relationship based on mutual respect, honesty, and a willingness to yield when an issue is in the other's area of expertise.

Firms have generally been creative at forging organizations that work for their situations. The important point is that there must be communication across the Pacific at various management levels and down to the working levels.

Operating Procedures

Organizational structures and reporting relationships are only the base from which decisions can be made and carried out. I recently noticed an article in *Nikkei Business* with the headline: "I've had it being the president of a *gaishi*." It was written by Shigeho Inaoka, who was the president of Nihon Apollo Computers. His dream of turning the organization into the leading workstation marketer in Japan was frustrated when his parent corporation in the United States, Apollo Computers, decided to merge with Hewlett Packard, in turn forcing a merger of the Japanese subsidiaries of both firms. While these things are a fact of life in business, Inaoka was insulted that he was notified about this dramatic event by a simple fax at about the time the merger was announced. He didn't even have enough time to forge a good response to the barrage of reporters who tried to contact him. Imagine what this did to the Japanese customer base and distributors, not to mention their own sales force. Though it is difficult to know who is to be blamed in this instance, it is clear that this mode of communication is suboptimal. Thus, within any organizational structure, one must determine the mode of communication across the Pacific at the various levels of the hierarchy. This is especially crucial in providing *anshinkan* to Japanese customers. When the Japanese subsidiary cannot solve a customer problem locally and the U.S. organization must be involved, it is a challenging but critical task to communicate the problem adequately and to secure a commitment on a date by which the problem will be resolved.

Defining and communicating problems must, of course, be reckoned with in any organization, but organizations that are cross-cultural have additional barriers to business communication. In communications between Japan and the United States, the first barrier is the time difference. Working across as many as twelve time zones leaves at most a few hours of overlap in business hours between the two countries. There is usually only one chance a day to resolve issues by telephone, and if the person called is not available, the problem may have to wait another day. Resorting to written communication exacerbates language problems, especially for the Japanese communicating in written English. Too little information may be provided, or the problem may not be presented clearly.

Problem-definition skills can greatly decrease decision-making turnaround time. Because of their schooling, Japanese employees must be trained to articulate problems and needs in the right manner. This is an area where cultural calibration is difficult. The Japanese often are either soft-spoken and don't verbalize problems or become so aggressive as to border on the abrasive. In one typical pattern, Japanese personnel demand that the U.S. parent change its methodology to what Japanese competition is doing. Most American managers tend to be much more receptive when the Japanese communicate a market need and allow the American manager the freedom to pick the methodology to meet it.

One workable communication mechanism is a regularly scheduled telephone conference on operating problems, with several levels of management present on both sides and an agenda agreed on in advance. Such conferences have two benefits. First, because managers at several levels attend, problems tend to be more crisply defined. For example, the communication does not depend on the English ability of one junior Japanese employee. Second, everyone hears the problem presented in the same manner and is aware of the commitments that have been made. When minutes of these conferences are used effectively, problems are likely to be resolved by the next conference. Even if such conferences are held no more than once a week, decisions that formerly took weeks and even months begin to be resolved.

Face-to-face meetings are inescapable in the business environment, particularly in cross-cultural communication, where much is done subtly, through facial expressions and body language. Senior managers of a Japanese subsidiary of an American firm fly to the United States frequently, sometimes as often as once a month. Regularly scheduled business and strategy reviews held on a quarterly basis are helpful. Higher-level issues, such as strategic direction and coordination, and major business decisions, such as new product introductions and addition of new partners, are the usual agenda; in addition, a regular agenda of such items as business indicators and schedules helps to provide continuity and to put ad-hoc topics in perspective. Unless one is very adept at dealing with meeting dynamics and politics, it is usually productive to visit the key decision makers in advance of the formal review to get approval of major proposals to be presented.

A liaison office in corporate headquarters that can work on problems during the subsidiary's normal business hours can also help communication. As long as the problem can be verbalized accurately, an eight-hour day can produce major progress on an issue. The only requirements for the success of this mechanism are that the personnel in the liaison office have both enough functional knowledge to address the problems and possible solutions intelligently and the social and personal capital needed to function in the headquarters organization. In my experience, those firms that have liaison staff with these characteristics are fortunate indeed.

IBM Corporation has taken a particularly interesting approach to this problem. In the mid-1980s, as Japan and its surrounding countries became of increasing importance, World Trade Corporation, the marketing arm of IBM, was reorganized from the two-pronged structure of AFE (America/Far East) and EMEA (Europe/Middle East/Africa) to the current three-pronged structure of AG (America Group), APG (Asia Pacific Group), and EMEA.

At the same time, IBM decided to move APG headquarters from New York to Tokyo, in part to allow IBM to retain control of its Japanese subsidiary while moving the decision-making authority close to the market so that decisions could be made expeditiously.

Those who remember that period in Tokyo know that this was a major investment. The APG was so large that there were not enough Western-style apartments in central Tokyo to accommodate the group, and rents rose. Several hundred people were moved to Tokyo, at a cost of perhaps several hundred thousand dollars each. Moreover, to head up the organization, a heavyweight—George Conrades—was brought in.

Frank Cary, former CEO of IBM, once asked rhetorically, "Can an elephant tapdance?" The truth of his affirmative answer was shown by the speed with which IBM entered and built a commanding position in the personal computer business. Perhaps the APG will prove to be another example, although the jury is still out on the question of whether it has increased Japanese customer satisfaction by shortening the turnaround time in solving problems.

· · ·

The Japanese often complain that foreign firms do not achieve the QCDS levels of Japanese firms. Tough customers tend not to be tolerant of that gap, despite the difficulties we have seen in matching, from across the ocean, what the best local firms can do. One might expect that Japanese employees of foreign firms would tend to favor foreign products, but often people who make their living by selling foreign products buy Japanese products for their own consumption. Perhaps a good test of the adequacy of a foreign firm's QCDS capability would be its success in winning over this group of people. Clearly, that would make the foreign firm a more attractive place to work and better motivate those who work there, a topic I discuss in the next chapter.

5

People: The Key to Intercultural Operations

MANY AMERICANS ASSUME that their Japanese subsidiaries operate like Japanese companies. To the contrary, the cultures of most foreign affiliate firms, even when staffed by Japanese, make them completely different from purely Japanese firms.

In a tightly coupled society, where heterogeneous elements tend to be put in separate categories rather than merged, concepts of insidership and outsidership are to be expected, although foreigners living in Japan may tire of being called *gaijin* (from *gai,* "outside," and *jin,* "person"). This is why foreign affiliate firms are referred to as *gaishi* (*shi* means "equity"). They look and feel very different from Japanese firms.

HUMAN RESOURCE SYSTEMS IN JAPAN AND THE UNITED STATES

The term *kaisha,* which was established by Abegglen and Stalk (1985) to designate the Japanese corporation, is used

117

here to refer to the typical large Japanese company. In order to contrast the *kaisha* and the *gaishi,* let me first examine the differences between the human resource systems of the *kaisha* and of the American firm operating in the United States.

Hiring Practices

The contrast begins with the inflow of human resources. For the most part, large Japanese corporations practice permanent employment, whereas most large American firms do not. In Japan, new college graduates enter a firm right after graduation and stay there until retirement. Lateral hiring from one company to another at the high levels is almost unknown. There are exceptions: Japanese firms anxious to diversify into new areas are beginning to hire laterally in order to acquire the new skills needed for success, and a few American firms such as IBM approximate the permanent employment practices of the Japanese firm. By and large, however, the hiring practices of the two cultures are markedly different, and it is important to understand the ramifications of these differences.

In the permanent employment set-up, there is only one method of entry into the organization: at the bottom, as a new college graduate. Partly because of the Japanese system of education, the recent college graduate is a blank—impressionable and moldable. The very frame of mind in which the young Japanese searches for a place of employment differs radically from that of the young American. In Japan, associating oneself with a prestigious firm is even more important for social credibility than for professional credibility: it facilitates marriage, financial assistance, and networking, among other things. In any case, Japanese companies rarely tell their new employees what their assignment is going to be.

Americans graduating from college look for something very different. Often they have developed an area of specialization, and corporations that want to hire them try to provide challenging entry-level positions that relate somewhat to their specialization. Unlike Japanese recent graduates, who expect to be in training for some time, American new employees try to use their theoretical knowledge to contribute to the firm's output as quickly as possible.

The differences are also apparent when the position does not turn out as expected. In the United States, the new college graduate tends to admit the error and move on. In most Japanese companies, however, it is the new employee's responsibility to conform to the new environment, altering his or her value system to become compatible with the firm. Often Japanese firms will have a new employee sign a letter of guarantee vowing that the employee will act consistently with the guidance of the firm; a guardian usually cosigns such a document as a guarantor, or *hoshonin*. Training programs for new employees are designed to provide an effective vehicle for making such an adjustment. It is not surprising, then, that the whole process leads to a homogeneous culture and a tightly coupled organization.

Lateral hiring—the means by which staffing is often done in American organizations—creates an opposite effect. When a firm places a highly ranked outsider in a managerial position, the lateral hire brings to the firm not only the needed skills but a whole new set of values that may be not at all like those of the organization—sometimes to the point where that lateral hire cannot cope and must leave the organization. Even when the new manager is successfully absorbed, his or her new values introduce a significant heterogeneity into the organization. Lateral hiring therefore contributes to the formation of a loosely coupled organization.

The new cultural values infused into a firm by lateral hiring can, of course, be important strategically. They might help to rejuvenate a stagnant organization. They might be necessary for success in a new business into which the firm is trying to diversify. Or the firm might be constantly in need of new ideas and new modes of operation. The tradeoff between a "pure blood" type of culture and a "mixed blood" culture largely depends on the factor critical for all effective organizations: the ability to focus when strategies and programs need to be executed effectively.

The Culture of the Workplace

Once in the Japanese organization, human resources are rotated, another factor that contributes to tight coupling. Firms are creative in the way they rotate their employees. An engineer who is transferred to manufacturing learns not only to develop products but to pay close attention to whether the product is easy or hard to manufacture. Placing a process engineer who has designed a manufacturing automation system in charge of executing his or her plan ensures that the employee plans realistically and regards the output of the project to be the successful execution of the plan, not simply a document to be passed to someone else. A salesperson who is transferred to the purchasing function is likely to be particularly aware of sales techniques employed by the people with whom he or she deals.

The culture of such an arrangement is fascinating and quite different from that of either an American corporation or a *gaishi.* An individual who is forced to live with the same set of, say, thirty people for perhaps three decades develops different attitudes and practices than someone in a situation with more mobility. The Japanese business culture has very strongly reinforced values, norms, and rituals, which are manifested in a variety of ways. First, there is the concept of *atarimae,* which roughly means "intuitively obvious" or "common sense." It represents that body of knowledge that the organization shares as its least-common-denominator mode of operation. Japanese organizations almost always have something called *shikitari,* the "way things are done around here," which makes any sort of free behavior seem out of place. When a superior in an organization says that doing something in a particular way is *atarimae,* very few people will ask, "Why?" This passive reaction is caused not by shyness, as most Westerners think, but by the risk of being seen as unfamiliar with the shared knowledge. The rules are not written down anywhere, and one must discover them for oneself and conform. For example, a junior employee of a Japanese company once told me that when she started out on her job, she had to learn informally that, on a trip away from the office, the junior employee is supposed to sit next to the taxi driver and pay the fare, arrange for a porter to pick up the luggage of the senior employees, and so on. One is supposed to do all this without being told, a difficult-to-translate concept called *a un no kokyu*. One must rely on one's sixth sense. It is about as far from spoon feeding as one can get.

In the United States, I was taught that anything is negotiable, but in Japan that principle seems not to apply to *atarimae*. Negotiating *atarimae* is either impossible or, at best, like pulling teeth. A particularly frustrating aspect for the foreigner is that in a discussion with a Japanese businessperson, the foreigner often finds agreement equated with familiarity with Japanese business practice; if there is disagreement, it is automatically assumed that the foreigner lacks understanding. The possibility that the foreigner is fully aware of Japanese practice but has a different perspective on the situation is simply not allowed for. This cultural mechanism can discourage the creativity that comes from challenging old assumptions.

A related aspect of the Japanese business culture is the harsh attitude toward individuality. Doing something according to one's own style is called *jikoryu,* a term that carries negative connotations. In the United States, even in fairly large organizations, a degree of individuality that produces good results is allowed and, in some high-technology firms, even encouraged. The astute manager who acts out of line, short-cutting the system in an intricate bureaucracy, may still be praised for obtaining fast results; the ends justify the means. Not so in Japan. In a recent course of negotiations, a U.S. firm wanted a clearer understanding of the terms the Japanese firm wanted and asked to have them stated in writing. One Japanese manager, who thought that the negotiations had gone on too long and that he knew what was needed, wrote the letter and sent it, greatly upsetting those in his organization who were not consulted. The result was right but the process wrong; and instead of being praised for his initiative in trying to move the discussion forward, he had to write an apology to all concerned. In this light, it can be seen why working "smart but short" hours is not effective in Japan. In fact, working inefficient but long hours is sometimes preferred.

The flip side of this situation is obviously the effective aspects of Japanese cooperation and teamwork. Like the Americans, I admire the Japanese in this area but for different reasons. Japan is the only Asian society whose large corporations have been able to separate group orientation from the family orientation derived from Confucian influence. Korea, for example, still has firms with over $10 billion in revenue run with significant influence from one or two families.

It is often said that the American corporate culture is additive, whereas the Japanese corporate culture is subtractive. In the United States, the new employee begins with zero points and accumulates points by producing results for the company. This approach, which requires initiative, risk taking, and a spirit of challenge, is reflected in the generous commission schemes that some American firms have for their salespeople. By contrast, the Japanese new employee begins with one hundred points, and points are deducted for snafus. That does not mean that Japanese employees and managers do not have to produce results; they do. But points are deducted for process-oriented mistakes, including cultural deviations. The ramifications for risk taking are significant.

Why do employees put up with such a system? The reason is simple. In Japan, isolation within an organization is almost worse than death, cutting one off from much of the flow of information and from the people network, the two elements that make an employee functional. Nevertheless, the lack of freedom the Japanese employee experiences is stressful, and so the system creates outlets for the stress that keep the employee from feeling overconstrained and discouraged. Unfortunately these mechanisms in the Japanese culture are the very elements that are the hardest for a foreigner to understand.

The first of these confusing means of alleviating stress is relativism. In Japan, nothing is absolute; everything is relative and situational. Good and bad are completely relative concepts. To a great extent, this relativism has to do with religion. Japan today is influenced by Shintoism, Buddhism, and Confucianism, all of which promote different values. In the business world, this relativism means that if one receives a certain response in a given situation, one cannot extrapolate to another similar set of circumstances and assume that the response will be the same. To the foreigner, this inability can seem quite illogical.

A second mechanism is a lubricating function in the relationships among people in an organization, who may have to live with each other for decades. One manifestation is the absence of the blunt no in the Japanese language. In order not to burn one's bridges, one has to express the negative in a subtle and soft manner. By contrast, the American yes and no are essential to communications among the heterogeneous people who live in the United States. More complex is the use of the *tatemae* and the *honne,* which foreigners tend to despise. In some contexts, the person who has been told the *tatemae* ("the official story") is supposed to be able to guess the *honne* ("the real story") from contextual information and to give the other person a break. Although the degree to which the Japanese culture uses this mode comes across to the American as a double standard, in light of the subtractive nature of evaluation the need for it is clear. The concepts of *tatemae* and *honne* exist in American business as well; the only difference is that one can read *honne* much better in one's own culture. The Japanese make much use of indirect language and unspoken communication techniques, and the foreigner often has trouble understanding Japanese facial expressions and body language. Moreover, in Japan the *honne* is only available in after-hours "personal" time.

This type of codified culture persists in Japan because the outflow of human resources from a firm is controlled. Large Japanese firms have low turnover rates, usually in the low single digits. The main outflow is from retirement at the predetermined age. This low turnover is significant for two reasons: information and operating methods rarely leak, and cultural values take hold and solidify. Both of these factors reinforce tight coupling.

STAFFING A *GAISHI:* MERGING CULTURES

Good people are the key to a successful business, but adhering to this obvious principle is no easy feat for a foreign firm in Japan. Several years ago, I gave a talk on recruiting new college graduates at the American Chamber of Commerce in Japan. The session was oversubscribed, and it was clear from the comments that human resource strategy was a common concern among the major *gaishi*s.

This is an example of another asymmetric problem: attracting and retaining good people is much harder for a Japanese subsidiary of an American firm—a *gaishi*—than for an American subsidiary of a Japanese firm. That was not always the case. Two decades ago, in Japan, working for a *gaishi* was "in." Back then, few people working for a Japanese firm had the opportunities for overseas travel available to a *gaishi* employee. Speaking English was a coveted skill. The United States was powerful, and its products and ideas were favored. By contrast, only a few years back, an American who went to work for a Japanese firm in Silicon Valley was somewhat negatively stigmatized.

Today the tables have turned. For the American, despite apprehensions about working for Japanese management, the stigma of working for a Japanese firm has diminished, partly as a result of Japanese success and partly because of America's tolerance of heterogeneity and differences in outlook and behavior. For the Japanese, the opportunities and skills formerly offered only by *gaishi*s are in abundance in Japanese firms. Given the strong cultural cohesion of the Japanese, it is not surprising that people who work for *gaishi*s are considered maverick Japanese. It is assumed that they either have misplaced loyalites or could not cope with the Japanese environment. Even employees of Japanese firms who come back to Japan from overseas assignments suffer from a weaker version of this stigma.

How, then, does one go about procuring human resources for a *gaishi?* As we have seen, many large Japanese firms hire predominantly new college graduates. The need for quick diversification has recently led to some lateral hiring, but in general midcareer job candidates are considered to be not quite "pure." By contrast, in the United

States considerable lateral hiring goes on. Headhunters gain reputations from finding a John Sculley to head Apple.

From a cross-cultural standpoint, this already suggests an asymmetry. A Japanese firm working through a U.S. headhunter can acquire the functional skills needed to get its U.S. operations going, and although not all the lateral hires may work out, the organization at least can start to function and provide return. A U.S. company trying to do business in Japan, however, might succeed in hiring a few experienced people—and there are *gaishi* job hoppers, who are to be avoided—but in order to grow, the organization must be staffed by new college graduates. As any experienced manager knows, getting tangible output from such new employees often takes longer than from lateral hires. It can be done, however, if one knows how to go about it and avoids some of the pitfalls.

Lateral Hiring

In the United States a firm in need of an experienced manager typically tries to hire someone from a competitor or from a firm in a related business. Most *gaishi*s need to adopt a similar approach in Japan in order to operate at a minimally competent level, particularly during the first five to ten years. The lures of compensation and position that work well in the United States, however, are by no means as effective in Japan. I have occasionally asked managers from *kaisha*s, apart from the context of recruiting, "Would a Japanese manager consider changing employers if offered three times his or her present pay?" The answer is either no or a very qualified yes, which usually means no in the Japanese culture.

The effective set of methods with which the Japanese harbor stability in their employment has developed over centuries. Their human resource policies originated in the operation of regional clans back in the days of the shoguns. Loyalty was then highly valued, of course; the Japanese still watch with awe when in a television drama a loyal clansman on his deathbed wishes well to the clan and its head, rather than his own family. At the same time, many Japanese like to operate in situations of restricted freedom. They like to be led instead of having to incur the responsibility and uncertainty of individual initiative.

Japanese *kaisha*s have capitalized on this tendency over a long period. In return for loyalty—including the willingness to relocate to any place the company chooses on a whim—they provide "cradle to grave" care. This includes support for all occasions like the birth of a child, marriage, and funerals, as well as financial support in the form of low-interest mortgages and other loans. Some of these financial handcuffs are not easy to shed. One begins to sense the power of the company when one sees the company logo not only on buildings, products, and stationery but also on credit cards, travel agency documents, and even the packets of sugar provided with coffee, as I saw in one Japanese firm. When one adds these forces to the social status and prestige of working for a well-known Japanese company, it is not surprising that the market supply of good human resources at the midcareer stage is limited.

Recently, however, my experience with Japanese recruitment firms is that more potential lateral hires are becoming available. For example, I recently came across a compilation of available midcareer candidates. Out of forty-eight entries, thirteen were from prestigious Japanese firms even a Westerner would find familiar. In general, they fall into two groups: the mavericks, different but excellent; and those who are seriously flawed. In the latter group are people who have had fights with their prior bosses, who have personal problems, or who lack patience or persistence; at the extreme is the *gaishi* hopper, who leaves a Japanese firm for a *gaishi* and continues to change firms every year or two. One obviously undesirable trait is an ego much greater than one's capability to perform, combined with unexpectedly strong defensive abilities. The less obvious fact is that there are many such people in Japan, where people are conditioned more to criticize and obstruct than to suggest and move forward. Thus there are few mavericks and many flawed, and needless to say, it is important to avoid the latter.

The mavericks are often uncovered through personal contacts and introductions. Again, through trust (the network of commitments), both the available person and the hiring firm are motivated to turn the situation into a positive-sum environment. There are examples of success through the headhunter channel as well, but it is important not to get stuck with someone whom a large Japanese company has found useless and asked a recruitment firm to help dump. Such people are losers, lacking drive, leadership skills, and managerial capability; they are worse than the famous *madogiwazoku*, the Japanese version of deadwood.

Once one has found an acceptable candidate, a few things must be carefully considered. Often convincing an experienced employee in a Japanese organization to sign on is only half the battle. In tightly coupled Japanese organizations, the employees of a firm are considered to belong to the firm at large, not just to a department; therefore, the loss of an employee is a serious threat to the department manager who oversees that employee. If the employee leaves, the department manager may have to submit a written apology to the company for losing a company resource. A manager will, therefore, fight tooth and nail to keep a valuable employee. If the employee considering leaving is young, the personnel department of the Japanese company (the present "guardian") may telephone his or her parents or other family members (the former guardian) to discuss the significant mistake being made and to seek their help in dissuading the employee from leaving. Obviously, such tactics require counterefforts, until the employee's departure from the Japanese firm is certain.

Good lateral hires often come from companies the *gaishi* works with. In Japan, it is not considered appropriate to hire such personnel, even if employees are dissatisfied with their current place of work. To do so would affect the working relationship between the firms. Companies therefore engage in subtle moves, such as arranging a temporary place of employment where the lateral hire works for a while before inconspicuously transferring into the originally intended firm.

Frequently the desire for short-term results motivates a foreign firm to hire an experienced manager—usually an unrealistic expectation. The effectiveness of a Japanese manager is often specific to the environment, a culture so strong that the manager needs significant deculturalization in order to be effective in another. And for the manager who departs a Japanese company, networking also ceases to operate in the same manner. The manager who no longer carries a business card from a prestigious company may begin to receive the cold shoulder. Finally, a Japanese manager is used to performing duties and achieving results with the group, with no one person taking the praise or blame. For someone from that environment, the possibility of turning things around singlehandedly in a new company is remote at best.

Let us look at two contrasting cases. In the first, a manager was hired from a *kaisha* into a first-line management position. His functional expertise was awesome, and people all over the organization consulted him. He brought his prior management culture with him, however, asking his subordinates to be loyal to him in return for being taken care of by him. He shouldered all the problems in his group, communicating neither problems outside the group to his subordinates nor problems within his group to his management. In a number of major projects that he handled, this style became untenable; yet it was so ingrained in him that he could not change it and eventually had to resign.

In another case, a worker was hired into a nonmanagerial position from a relatively small Japanese firm. He had a direct communication style—one that often rubs people the wrong way. His functional expertise was good, however, and his pragmatism in problem solving was respected by many. Although he was not an easy person to manage because of his strong views on many issues, he did well and has since risen to the ranks of management.

As is the case almost anywhere in the world, the higher the position one wishes to fill through lateral hiring, the greater the risk the employee will not work out. That phenomenon is compounded in Japan, where the culture of the *gaishi* contrasts sharply with the strong culture of the *kaisha*. Therefore, although candidates for lateral hiring are becoming more readily available, it is important to avoid the *gaishi* hopper and to assess the cultural adjustment that must take place in order for functional expertise to bear fruit in the new environment.

Recruiting New College Graduates

As a *gaishi* moves into the second phase of its maturity, it must start to hire new college graduates. Even this is an uphill battle, however. As I discussed earlier in this chapter, new college graduates in Japan look for very different things than do their counterparts in the United States. The Japanese student generally looks not for a specific job but for a compatible environment. Association with a brand-name company is important to various social aspects of one's life, including marriage. A large and well-known enterprise is also considered desirable because of the paternalism of Japanese firms. The graduating student leaves the guardianship of the parents and enters the guardianship of the company, which is expected to continue the guidance and education provided by the parents. Though American students have similar concerns, they are adventurous about going with young, dynamic firms if the trade-off is that they can try something new and exciting that a more established firm cannot provide.

Japanese students prefer stability. This is another manifestation of *anshinkan*. When foreign companies ask Japanese students why they are not immediately attracted by the opportunities presented by foreign firms, they quickly point out that they are afraid of layoffs and pullouts. In the United States, switching jobs in midcareer is acceptable, and employees can afford to take risks.

Also important is the difference between transactional employment and a longer-term relationship between employer and employee. The former concept is often dominant in the United States in knowledge-intensive service industries such as investment banking and consulting. The firm pays for individual know-how combined with an enormous—sometimes unsustainable—effort on a short-term basis, and the output is ruthlessly measured. This kind of arrangement is attractive to some Americans because of the challenges inherent in such a strenuous situation and because the compensation is usually very high. It does not work well in Japan, however, except in focused and specific cases. Students join a company for the long haul, and employers do not expect output for the first few years.

The asymmetry is even clearer when one considers what it takes to attract new college graduates. There is far from a free market in hiring. When one telephones a renowned university in Japan to ask about the process of recruiting and hiring new graduates, one is given a party line on the rules: new employees start work in April, after graduation; and recruitment begins the preceding July. That is what one is told; the fact, however, is that by July the game is over.

Established Japanese firms start unofficial recruiting activity as early as April, one year prior to the start of work. Personnel staff members as well as reputable managers who are graduates of good universities get in touch with professors at their former schools. Usually these professional relationships are longstanding and may have included donation of equipment, joint research projects, and the like. The professors play an important role in recruitment. Japanese students go to their professors for *shushoku shidoh* ("employment guidance")—another form of *shidoh*. This is basically where the student's desires and capabilities are matched with the available positions. This *shidoh* is much stronger than career guidance in the American sense; a student who goes against the *shidoh* limits his or her career opportunities. The professor's commitment is also strong. One professor told me, "I wouldn't send my student to a firm I wouldn't send my son to." He also gave me examples of situations in which he would intervene if it became evident, even a few years after graduation, that one of his graduates had been placed in the wrong firm, and would try to find that student a new place of employment.

Thus, it makes sense for *gaishi*s to approach professors. Recently, however, a consortium of foreign firms in Japan banded together and tried to approach such professors as a coalition. The initial calls were reminiscent of cold sales calls: unreturned phone messages, no-show appointments, appointments too short to accomplish anything, and standard pitches by professors that conveyed no useful information. Building a relationship in this context takes a long time.

The other challenge is that a critical factor in the relationship between the school and the firm is stability in the number of students hired each year. American firms often hire on a "feast or famine" basis. This makes sense from a managerial standpoint: when times are good, one can afford to add people; and when times are bad, one must cut back. But it is not how things work in Japan. Although the number of available openings varies from year to year, seldom does a renowned Japanese firm fail to hire anyone in a given year unless that firm is in serious trouble—in itself an unattractive signal to students.

Through the contacts with professors, the best Japanese students from the best Japanese universities are given *naitei*s ("informal commitments") by July of the year before they graduate, when technically one should not even have started the hiring process. It might seem, therefore, that the prospects for *gaishi*s to hire good new graduates are dim. The question remains, however, whether people hired through this process are really appropriate for the *gaishi*. Fortunately, there are ways to attract high-quality college graduates by targeting the right segment of the student population. An increasing number of students either are interested in trying something nontraditional or do not find the Japanese lifetime commitment appealing. Because the Japanese culture is so strong, it is clear that such students are a different breed from those who opt for a more routine career. This is the start of the bias against the maverick Japanese.

Foreign firms offer many attractive features to the new college graduate, including quicker opportunity for contribution at a young age, individual consideration, tolerance of speaking out, an international perspective, an open-door policy, performance-oriented compensation systems, tolerance of risk taking, and less sex discrimination. With traditional Japanese, these arguments seem to fall on deaf ears, but to the maverick Japanese they make good sense.

The continuing debate is whether foreign firms should target these mavericks or go for more traditional Japanese

135

employees despite poor yields in the hiring process. From my experience, it is clear that the mavericks adjust to the culture of an American firm better than do the traditional students. At the same time, however, I have often found that the behavior of the mavericks tends to cause friction with important customers and partners who have more traditional Japanese values. Thus, it seems that there must be a mixture of the two kinds of employees, provided one can attract good prospects in the traditional category.

Recruiting the mavericks among new college graduates requires methods totally different from those used to hire traditional graduates. The process is more Westernized. One sends direct mailers and places advertisements in recruiting magazines, providing reply cards. Those who answer are invited to an event such as a seminar at which prospecting and informal screening take place. Company visits follow; and if there is a match, an informal offer is extended. Again, all this has to happen before July if one is to have a chance at good candidates.

How do such new employees work out? My experience is that being successful in the *gaishi* correlates better with the characteristics of the individual than with anything else. Among the mavericks, some are extremely aggressive; in a few cases such people have begun producing within a year or two, even in areas as tough as sales. Thus, as long as one targets the right type of people and trains and motivates them appropriately, hiring new college graduates may not be as long-term a proposition as one might think.

An Example of Effective Segment-Oriented Hiring

Every year, the Japanese newspapers publish a list of the companies new college graduates most want to work for. For years the list was the same, and IBM Japan was the only *gaishi* to appear near the top (usually in the top ten); one had to look much farther to find Fuji Xerox and perhaps one other *gaishi*. Recently Nihon DEC has been rising rapidly in popularity and is becoming recognized as a success story at hiring in Japan.

As recently as the early 1980s, many Japanese students considered Digital Equipment Corporation (DEC)—a company specializing in minicomputers—to be a watch company. At the time Nihon DEC made the decision to break with its past and pursue an aggressive staffing plan to build a strong technical organization essential to success in the system business. The rapid increase in personnel indicates that the company focused on that area. Sales followed; and as a result, DEC is now aiming to become one of the top five computer manufacturers in Japan, after Fujitsu, NEC, IBM Japan, and Hitachi. Around this time, DEC aggressively started to approach Japanese universities. The first year they got zero students. The second year they got zero students. By 1989–90 they were hiring three hundred new college students a year.

To build the necessary staff, DEC used the following hiring strategies:

- "Feast or famine" hiring of new college graduates stopped, and relatively stable hiring began, which im-

137

parted a sense of *anshinkan* to both students and faculty—the prospects and their advisors.

- The hiring effort was started early in the cycle—the April prior to the April when new employees start work.
- More than six thousand packets of color brochures and other literature were sent to professors and students.
- Two hundred visits were paid to universities.
- A two-page ad was placed in *Beruf,* a recruitment magazine used to draw leads from interested students.
- Desirable students were invited to a three-week series of technical seminars.
- The company's image as a desirable social environment was upgraded. Two books were published about DEC, and promotional material was sent to parents of prospective new employees, focusing on employee education.

This list does not exhaust all possible hiring strategies, yet these steps have brought DEC a significantly enhanced image in the new-employee marketplace. The approach allows for some self-selection. No amount of publicity or effort will divert a student who is linked with a professor and aspires singlemindedly to work for a prestigious Japanese firm. Instead, DEC effectively reaches those students who are not likely to be satisfied working with a large Japanese company. One effective tactic DEC has used with interested students is the so-called job selection system, which allows new employees to choose the job categories they would like to work in. Most Japanese companies, as we have seen, assign new employees to jobs according to the convenience of the firm.

DEC also works through other channels to find good

people from specialized segments, such as the female population. One interesting phenomenon in the popularity charts I mentioned is that *gaishi*s have been gaining significant favor with female students, who perceive that *gaishi*s treat women more equitably than do male-dominated Japanese firms. Both DEC and IBM Japan have gone after this segment. DEC has also targeted Japanese graduates of American universities, another distinctive segment. The combined efforts DEC has made require commitment, but they have been successful in procuring for DEC the resource perhaps most difficult to obtain but most important for running an effective business.

MOTIVATING LOCAL EMPLOYEES IN A *GAISHI*

Few employees of Japanese firms criticize or complain outwardly about their own firms. Of course, after hours and over drinks, one hears grumbling, but it is subdued. Part of the reason for this discretion is the tightly coupled nature of the Japanese firm; explicit complaining, when caught, leads to excommunication. By contrast, *gaishi* employees are outspoken about inconsistencies and problems in their own firms.

As we have seen, the differences found in the Japanese environment between purely Japanese firms and *gaishi*s stem largely from the wide differences in value systems between the two countries. These differences are reflected in various issues that relate to the motivation of Japanese employees in a *gaishi*.

The Value System of the *Gaishi*

Most people are influenced significantly by their up-bringing and tend to respect values they have learned from their parents and from school. A *gaishi,* because of its strong involvement with the parent corporation, must operate with hybrid values, which Japanese customers and partners as well as employees may find objectionable in their tightly coupled society.

Some *gaishi*s try to operate with the same set of values as the parent company. From the American standpoint, it is natural to want a consistent value system functioning worldwide as an informal control mechanism; otherwise, every interaction between headquarters and its overseas subsidiary becomes a complex cultural problem that leads to misunderstandings and adds to overhead. Yet although most people I have met in Japanese subsidiaries say they abide by the values of their parent corporations, they usu-ally have not internalized these values. As a result, they rarely know how to apply the values in practical situations unless they have strong local role models. I have seen few *gaishi* presidents able both to embody values that work in the United States and successfully to transplant them as is to the Japanese workplace.

I believe that a better way to go is to understand the position of the *gaishi*—interacting on the one hand with headquarters and on the other with customers, distribu-tors, partners, licensees, and internally with employees—and to forge a value system the employees can work with while minimizing head-on conflict with headquarters. Sometimes this is very difficult, and in that situation my suggestion is to choose values that lead to maximum business success for the *gaishi,* rather than using the satisfaction of either the parent corporation or the customer as the criterion.

Compensation Systems

Performance appraisal and compensation systems also tend to reflect cultural differences. Most of the pure motivational and performance appraisal schemes used by American firms create enormous problems of execution in the *gaishi* environment. Specifically, the results-oriented appraisal system currently in vogue in the United States is in sharp contrast with Japanese practice, which emphasizes seniority.

The first issue is the time frame within which an employee is expected to produce results. Although there are exceptional Japanese who start carrying their own weight in the first year, most are not conditioned to do so. In one Japanese semiconductor company, the training program for new college graduates begins by having them run ten times around a lake for the first few weeks, to teach them persistence, patience, and humility. Next, anxious though they may be to learn about products and technologies, they spend several weeks learning to work harmoniously with people senior to them. They then learn about manufacturing, not in a classroom but at a station on the plant floor that performs a simple operation. They also may be sent out to help retailers sell products from other divisions of the company. An impatient businessperson might consider these activities a waste of time, but in Japan such methods are seen as important in establishing the right expectations in the minds of the employees and indoctrinating them into the culture. This type of training, which develops patience and lowers the expectations of the new employee, results in fewer complaints later on.

One Japanese academic has said that a career in a Japanese firm is a marathon, whereas an American career is a series of 100-meter dashes. In engineering-related functions, some Japanese firms do not grant the formal title of engineer until an employee has spent five years on the job and passed an examination. When one's career in a firm spans four decades, there is no need to produce results early on. Recall the Japanese concept of *shugyo*, in which an apprentice must wait years before receiving positive feedback.

Most *gaishi*s cannot afford this kind of time frame. Many have reasonable training programs, but these programs tend to be short. Moreover, most departments are so understaffed that many new employees are plunged into work without much guidance. That raises a highly controversial issue: whether compensations should be based on performance and results or on seniority and effort, with results being an important but secondary consideration.

*Gaishi*s vary widely in their practices in this area. Some pay according to seniority, as is done in Japanese firms. Others hover at the opposite extreme, using the same performance-based compensations system as the parent firm. The latter scheme can work, but in my experience it causes stress in the organization because of the limitations the cross-cultural environment places on it.

The first constraint on a performance-based system is that performance evaluation usually involves individualized goal-setting. In Japanese society, it is rare for one person to receive praise or humiliation for the results of a project. People enter a firm as a group of new college graduates (such as the class of 1990), and band together as a group. They often share information about salary increases with each other. Since there is a strong bias in the Japanese culture to interpret fairness as equality (*byodo* in Japanese), fair differentiation of pay is a hard concept for the Japanese to understand early in their careers. Thus, they always have concerns about the criteria for differentiation based on individual performance; such differentiation goes against the tendency for tight coupling within the group. As a result, many *gaishi*s in Japan use a hybridized compensation scheme in which pay is based on seniority during the first few years; in later years, performance plays a heavier role. In other words, new Japanese college graduates need a few years of deconditioning after their sixteen years of Japanese education and its emphasis on equality and harmony.

The sales commission is another controversial form of compensation. Some American corporations motivate their salespeople by raising the proportion of their compensation that comes from commissions in relation to the base. This type of scheme causes problems in the Japanese environment. First, sales cycles are often longer in Japan than in the United States, and a commission incentive limits management's flexibility in changing account and territorial assignments; special compensation may have to be considered for missionary work. Second, a salesperson would tend to sacrifice long-term issues for short-term gain—not a practice favored by Japanese management. Third, since closing a purchase order is considered a team effort, a windfall going to one person is likely to be considered unfair. For these reasons, many *gaishi*s pay their salespeople commissions but make the incentive pay a much smaller proportion of the total compensation compared with their U.S. counterparts.

The second problem with a performance-based appraisal scheme is evaluating real functional ability versus language and cultural ability. I recall a situation in which a Japanese employee reported to two bosses, one American and one Japanese. The Japanese boss felt that while the employee's English skills and ability to get along with foreigners were excellent, his job skills were below par. The American boss considered that in comparison with others who could not even communicate, much less resolve issues in a businesslike manner, the employee was effective. In fact, the employee was considered a bit of a maverick by his colleagues, a factor the American probably did not understand. I have often heard Japanese employees with more traditional values complain of mavericks who do little work but look good when they put together a presentation. For that reason, I hold many meetings in Japanese, in order to separate language ability from job-related ability; but not all foreign managers can afford to do so.

Another constraint on the evaluation of results relates to the generalist role the employee is expected to take in the firm. The Japanese educational system biases learning toward generalization rather than specialization, and the Japanese corporate environment tends to reinforce this bias with its rotation programs. More important, customers expect *gaishi* employees to be able to handle questions and problems in wide-ranging areas of expertise; "that's not my job" doesn't cut it. Therefore an employee may be assigned to work in an area other than the one originally intended or ultimately planned.

Yet another issue involves priorities. American employees are expected to manage their time according to the importance of their tasks. If there is not enough time to do everything, low priority tasks are cut. In Japan, the huge network of human relationships makes it difficult to avoid small favors that may wind up taking a great deal of time. Moreover, in a society where tasks are personalized—one must communicate, apologize, and congratulate in person, rather than over the telephone—things take time, and much of this time is spent after work. The result is that people work unreasonably long hours, and effort has to become one measure of performance appraisal.

The final issue has to do with output that is not in phase with input: that is, an employee may have been assigned a task during one review cycle, and the results may show up after he or she has been transferred to another department. How does one give credit to a person who is not directly involved at the time of the completion of the project? In a *gaishi* tightly controlled by headquarters, there is also the possibility that the performance of the local employee has been limited by headquarters policy—for example, a course correction or cancellation of a project for reasons beyond the employee's control.

These issues are no doubt serious considerations in the performance appraisal process in American firms in the United States as well. The point is that in the Japanese environment the problems are compounded, because fairness across groups is such an important emotional point.

The importance of fairness also explains why certain

well-intentioned moves by *gaishi*s are not always appreciated. One example is their approach to relocating employees. Japanese firms transfer employees without giving them any choice in the matter, even when the only option is to relocate a father alone for several years. *Gaishi*s—like their American parent firms—tend to be more tolerant. They nudge people to relocate but consider backing off if personal hardship is involved. Such consideration is rarely appreciated because other, more emotional issues often take precedence.

One of the challenges of managing Japanese employees is this sort of emotional caretaking. Again, the importance of nonverbal communication arises. In the United States, a disgruntled employee can have a sizable confrontation with his or her manager, and the two parties can aim to resolve the differences on the table. Afterward, the emotions can simmer down in a reasonably short period of time. As a manager in Japan, one must be very sensitive to a phenomenon called *hesomage* (literally, "bending the belly button"), where a Japanese employee has been emotionally hurt, but doesn't say anything. It is up to the manager to find out—sometimes quite a challenge—and managers vie for this information by going drinking with their subordinates after hours. When this phenomenon is persistently ignored, a manager can be in the amazing situation of having a Japanese subordinate abruptly quit and never mention the real reason for leaving. By then, recovery is close to impossible.

The Issue of Expatriates

Expatriates also tend to provoke emotion. American employees who are transferred from headquarters to work in a local subsidiary are often considered necessary but not always desirable.

The expatriate is asked to work far from home, in a country in which he or she may not feel comfortable. In order to compensate for the imposition and to create an environment in which the employee can be productive, the *gaishi* provides many allowances, including housing, goods, and services, in an attempt to create living conditions that come as close as possible to those the employee is used to at home.

In the case of Japan, this comfortable environment is usually one a local employee cannot even hope to acquire. As has been mentioned, many Japanese live in what they call rabbit houses, whereas foreign managers live in specially designed apartments, in choice areas with layouts comparable to Western houses and rents that can easily exceed $10,000 per month. An expatriate employee had better show significant value added and output to the subsidiary for the local employees to feel that this is fair. If anyone believes that expatriate compensations can be kept secret from local employees, let me say that every employee of a *gaishi* I have asked has told me that most locals know what an expatriate's fringe benefits are costing the company.

Another aspect of this differentiated treatment is that it excludes the expatriate employee from most average Japanese interactions. Many expatriate employees I know

147

would rather spend their time at a Western social club, for example, than at an *akachochin* bar, where low-salaried employees exchange bottom-line opinions over drinks. Part of the problem here is on the Japanese side: the interactions are so culture-bound that one cannot fully take part in them without having practically grown up in Japan. But that does not excuse the expatriate from trying to become part of such situations.

Despite these problems, the expatriate makes three contributions to the local subsidiary. First, the more the U.S. headquarters wishes to control the local subsidiary, the more important become communication skills, including the ability to cope with headquarters politics. My experience has been that a Japanese employee who has not grown up in the United States, or at least had significant experience there, will not have the necessary intercultural skills—in particular, assertiveness—to fight for the required resources, support, or policies from headquarters.

The second contribution the expatriate makes to the *gaishi* is functional skills and the ability to train local employees in a functional area. As we have seen, hiring and training new college graduates is a long-term proposition. Even lateral hiring requires that the new employee go through significant deculturization and training before becoming productive. These functional holes must somehow be filled, and expatriates are often used for this purpose.

Finally, expatriates are key when it comes to aiding headquarters in making the right global decisions. Expatriates can represent local interests in the context of global strategies and can be instrumental in making the proper trade-offs between the two often-conflicting factors. Local employees tend by their nature to be biased toward localization.

My own view is that expatriates will always be needed for these three reasons. In view of the high expense involved, they should be used strategically and aggressively. At the same time, expatriates should find ways to immerse themselves in the lives of the local employees and train locals in the intercultural and functional skills that will be needed as the subsidiary matures and more autonomy becomes necessary.

Perhaps it is becoming clear why *gaishi* employees are more open to criticizing their firms than are employees of Japanese firms. The former are, in fact, under enormous pressure, sandwiched between two cultures and having to serve two masters who are often in conflict, the U.S. parent corporation and the Japanese customer. In addition, they are always comparing the *gaishi* as a work environment with its Japanese competitors. It may be a case of the grass being greener on the other side of the fence, because many *gaishi* employees have never worked in a purely Japanese firm. I recall one *gaishi* employee who frequently complained about his company cafeteria until one day he was taken to a Japanese customer's cafeteria and was amazed to find that it had not been renovated for decades.

On the other hand, the credibility of local management makes a legitimate difference in the comparison *gaishi* employees make with respect to *kaisha* employees. When a Japanese subsidiary is managed too centrally by the U.S. parent, employees tend to view local management simply as puppets of U.S. corporate management and not as empowered managers. There is also a reasonable correlation between *gaishi*s that are functionally decentralized and those that have a more Japanized culture, since this by and large determines how much decision-making capability can reside in Japan.

It pays for foreign firms to be sensitive to issues affecting local employees as they make decisions regarding their Japanese subsidiary. Too many *gaishi*s are staffed with employees who are only half committed to the goals of the firm. With that level of commitment, competing against the *kaisha* is clearly going to be a losing battle. There are, fortunately, some *gaishi*s that have squarely tackled the problems. Let us look at one example.

A Hybridized Human Resource System: The Example of IBM Japan

IBM Japan recently celebrated its fiftieth anniversary. Started as a maintenance and sales function, it has over the years added manufacturing plants, development facilities, and the ability to develop new local products. As a result, it has a multibillion-dollar level of revenue per year and recognition as an excellent *gaishi*.

IBM Japan's human resources system represents a careful mixture of systems and values used by IBM worldwide and those that fit well with the Japanese culture. This represents one approach to the motivational problems described earlier in this chapter. In the area of compensation, IBM Japan uses a hybridized seniority-merit system closer to what Japanese corporations practice than the more aggressive performance/results–oriented scheme American firms are used to. Until an employee reaches supervisory level, seniority plays a key role in determining pay increases. Once an employee reaches the manager level, merit takes on a much more important role in compensation. IBM Japan also sets compensation to be competitive with its Japanese rivals rather than with other *gaishis*, and the thirty-seven types of benefit it offers its employees are oriented more toward conventional Japanese practice, including health, housing, education, insurance, and sports and recreation subsidies.

In the area of culture, IBM Japan has forged its own values and methodologies by judiciously mixing aspects of the IBM culture with Japanese organizational practices. It has adopted such IBM values as respect for the individual, an open-door policy, emphasis on customer service, and quality. At the same time, it practices a more consensus-oriented decision-making style relative to its parent company, allows the use of Japanese in communications at the lower levels of the organization, and has adopted lapel pins, which are often used by Japanese firms to instill a sense of belonging and identity.

With respect to training, IBM Japan has adopted the fervor with which the IBM Corporation pursues people development. IBM Japan is said to invest many times what its Japanese competitors spend on the development of its personnel. It has a layered education approach, divided into new employees, managers, and senior management. It also offers educational assistance and subsidies for studying at foreign universities.

Although it represents a merging of the two cultures and systems, IBM Japan's business style is somewhat different from that of its parent corporation. Managers in IBM Japan must try to bridge the gap; their credo is "Sell Japan to IBM; sell IBM to Japan."

Human resources policy in a *gaishi* really tests the ability to operate between two cultures. Good QCDS capability and international problem-solving infrastructure need proper motivation and people to run them. On the other hand, addressing the issues discussed in this chapter will go a long way toward helping one become a semi-insider in Japan. In the next chapter, I shall discuss how to nurture people in both U.S. headquarters and the Japanese subsidiary to make them effective in the global environment.

6

The Globalization of Human Resources

IN THE INTERNATIONAL BUSINESS context, a special type of human resource has become crucial—the global executive, at both upper and mid-level in the organization. According to a recent article in *Fortune* ("How to Be a Global Manager," 1988) the global executive is equally at home in and can transact business equally effectively in, say, Tokyo and New York City. The need for such executives, the article claimed, will increase substantially toward the end of the century.

I happen to be as comfortable living in Boston or Silicon Valley as in Tokyo, to name just a few places, and in fact have tackled business problems in all these places. I agree that global executives are essential, for two reasons. First, as the last three chapters described, the constant balancing and interaction between global and local factors in decision making affects the corporate commitment to penetrate a market such as Japan. Global executives influence the corporation to make the right set of tradeoffs and produce the right business results. Often decisions are made based on facts and assumptions that feel comfortable in one en-

153

vironment but may not be optimal for the entire corporation. Second, given the cultural differences outlined in the first three chapters, it is easy to see how global executives play a crucial role in the day-to-day problem solving involved in penetrating the Japanese market.

Not only will the demand for global executives undoubtedly grow exponentially over time, but we are already suffering from a severe shortage in the supply of such human resources. Silicon Valley firms need many such people in order to sell to or trade with the Japanese and to compete effectively with Japanese firms. On the other side, in all my trans-Pacific business dealings, I have met only a handful of Japanese who can come across effectively to a Westerner.

CHARACTERISTICS OF THE GLOBAL EXECUTIVE

The global executive must be able to articulate and communicate cross-culturally. Of course, being perfectly bicultural—being able to behave natively in two cultural contexts—is ideal. Unlike countries within Europe, however, the United States and Japan are so far apart culturally that bicultural people are virtually nonexistent. That fact implies that developing a pool of bicultural people is the wrong goal; it would probably not yield enough people to fill the need.

Although speaking multiple languages is helpful, being competent internationally is not directly related to language skills. Linguistically, there is a vast difference between syntax and semantics. I have met many Japanese people who, though able to construct perfect English sentences, leave Americans at a loss to know what they mean because they have simply translated into English the indirect expression they would have used in Japanese. For example, a Japanese engineer recently testifying in the U.S. courts regarding a possible copyright infringement was asked by a U.S. attorney, "Did you examine and use the copyrighted software in your development efforts?"

The engineer responded, "I don't think so."

Immediately the U.S. attorney demanded, "What do you mean—you don't know?"

In fact, in Japanese the expression the engineer used tends to mean, "No, I did not."

Americans often need to hear things directly. I know a Japanese manager who can speak almost no English, yet his Japanese is so well organized and clearly stated that when he speaks through an interpreter, Americans have no problem understanding him. Who is more internationally effective, the Japanese who can form grammatically correct but incomprehensible English sentences or the one who can speak only Japanese but who can be clearly understood through a translator? International effectiveness starts with the ability to communicate across cultures.

When it comes to intercultural communication, my experience suggests that Americans tend to have the advantage. American society requires people from different backgrounds to communicate, and the only way to do so is to be clear and direct. Add to this the importance that Americans place on open debate, and it becomes clear that those who wish to succeed in American business have to acquire clear communications capability. The problem with many American managers usually has more to do with excessive tenacity in holding to one's native values and an inadequate sensitivity to other cultures and ways of doing business.

The Japanese have a different problem. Neither their educational system nor their society encourages articulation. Communication in the Japanese classroom is often a one-way lecture by the teacher. When there is an exchange, students are usually asked questions to which they memorized the answers the night before. They have few opportunities to verbalize complex thoughts that need structured articulation. When I teach new college graduates in Japan, I am always astonished at their lack of ability in this area.

The indirectness of the Japanese language is not a help either. In fact, when Japanese managers in a *gaishi* were allowed to write performance appraisals for their subordinates in Japanese, some of the managers with the worst English preferred to write the appraisals in English, claiming it was an easier language in which to give feedback.

At the other extreme, the Japanese perhaps don't realize that it actually takes practice to be articulate. Recently, prompted by the controversial book *The Japan That Can Say No,* more Japanese are trying to be direct. This is a positive trend, but Japanese directness still comes across awkwardly, because the speakers have had no practice. This is another instance where cultural calibration is difficult. Japanese sometimes overreact, becoming either insulting or inaccurate. The book itself unfortunately suffers from these very mistakes. Still, it is a start.

Also, in a Japanese organization, where career advancement depends more on not making mistakes than in the United States, it is important to remain *happobijin* ("pretty to everyone"). Taking clear positions risks friction with someone. In the United States taking a position is positive, because the objective is to get others to see things one's way. Consider the Frank Sinatra hit "My Way," which says much about American individualism.

Growing up in Japan, I was a relatively quiet person. When I went to the United States to complete my education, I experienced a rude awakening: nothing happens until one speaks out. Prep school, MIT, Harvard Business School, and Intel all strongly encouraged and at times forced me to be vocal; but given my previous conditioning in Japan, it took me nearly a decade to acquire this capability. The change became evident when I returned to work in Japan; the facial expressions and body language of the people around me clearly showed resentment toward the overt and direct expressions I had acquired in the United States. And I am not alone. Employees of Japanese firms who have been transferred to foreign subsidiaries share this sense as they try to readjust to their own culture. They have somehow become "weird": they are too outspoken, they have allowed their Japanese to get "out of tune," they have gotten out of synch with the subtle, unwritten code of behavior. It is surely a sign of the strength of Japanese culture when one finds people discriminating against their own compatriots who have been transferred, perhaps even unwillingly, to a foreign country.

The extent of this cultural cohesion is unique to Japan. As mentioned earlier, other, less-developed Asian nations, especially those with newly industrialized economies, have a much larger proportion than does Japan of educated people who speak English, mainly because those societies don't exclude people who have come under foreign influence. Korea, for example, has been extremely active in recruiting repatriated Koreans, whether from foreign universities or firms, although the trend has recently slowed somewhat. In attracting these repatriates, large Korean firms offer significant positions and compensation packages, something Japanese firms would never consider doing lest it hurt the delicate balance and harmony in their organizations. So this type of international vitalization rarely occurs in a Japanese organization.

A second key characteristic of global executives—as important as the first—is an open mind. They need the courage to expose themselves to new ideas and to try to understand others' points of view. I recall an American expatriate manager who did not bother to learn Japanese and who spent much of his spare time at the Tokyo American Club. Under normal circumstances, he would have been a disaster, but owing to his listening skills, his open mind, and his ability to react to what he heard, the Japanese businesspeople he dealt with were talking about his effectiveness years after he was transferred back to the United States.

In this context, though it is important to listen to foreigners and to try to understand them, using one's own logic, it is even more important to try to understand *why* they say certain things. In the West, efficiency is generally considered a virtue; but the Japanese orientation to people often means that harmony is given precedence over efficiency. Therefore, accepting the surface meaning of a Japanese person's statement without probing the underlying thought process is likely to result in surprises later on, when one finds out that the initial understanding was based on a false assumption. The logical thought process is not different but the underlying reason may be interpreted incorrectly or some other important factor may be missed.

For example, I recall a meeting between representatives of a U.S. firm and those of a Japanese firm that wished to license a piece of technology from the American firm. The Americans asked the Japanese to divulge how they would be using the technology, so as to decide how to administer and control the flow of technology, but the Japanese party was not accommodating. The U.S. party read their reluctance as lack of cooperation and failure to respect intellectual property.

Sensing a lack of communication, I took one of the key members of the Japanese group aside and asked him, in Japanese, why they were unwilling to provide the information. After some probing, it became evident that their only worry was that the U.S. firm might use the information as leverage in renegotiating the price of the technology. In fact, the pricing had basically been agreed upon; and when I guaranteed that the U.S. team would not use the information for that purpose, the Japanese immediately put together a list of the proposed uses.

A third characteristic of the global executive, and one hard to come by, is the ability to make the right tradeoffs between pragmatism and cultural sensitivity. Many Japanese companies will reject a proposal from a *gaishi* by saying that it does not show enough understanding of Japan, when in fact they do not want to admit that the proposal does not sit well with them personally. It therefore takes tremendous courage to pursue a creative idea that has worked in the United States and can indeed be transplanted to Japan. Robert Christopher cites a good example in his book *Second to None* (1986). When the

American Family Life Insurance Company initially conceived of marketing cancer insurance policies, most prospective Japanese partners tried to discourage the effort. The firm plunged ahead by setting up a Japanese branch; and ten years later, it held a 70-percent share in a market with more than a dozen competitors.

On the other hand, if a U.S.-originated idea will not work in Japan, one has to be able to put one's foot down and risk being perceived as a negative thinker. The important point here is to be able to articulate the reasons that the idea will not work in Japan, in terms culturally acceptable to an American. A reason must be clearly stated (not just that it goes against Japanese culture); otherwise, American managers, some of whom think that anything goes, will not be convinced, and one will simply appear to be unsupportive of others' ideas. For example, it must be explained why tossing out a completely new idea at the bargaining table, and expecting an immediate reaction, is unproductive in Japan. The tightly coupled Japanese tend to make decisions in teams, and their group discussion can take place only away from the bargaining table.

Creativity is essential to the global executive. One of the biggest obstacles in solving business problems in the international context is the feeling that cultural limitations place more constraints on a decision in a foreign country than would be true in a domestic situation. Creativity is needed to transcend this obstacle. In a typical situation, a series of discussions comes to a standstill because of inertia on the Japanese side. The American becomes frustrated; in the United States, it would take only a telephone call to a counterpart in the other firm to find out what is going on. But working within a familiar international culture usually allows more degrees of freedom than one might have in a domestic situation. A creative person can look at a problem from a different angle, change the rules of the game, and come up with a win-win solution. Usually the proposal will be quickly adopted: by the Americans because it is innovative and helps break an impasse; and by the Japanese because they have an easier time accepting even risky solutions from someone outside their organizations, so that if the proposal fails they do not have to pinpoint the culprit.

I once intervened when a relationship between an American company and a Japanese company was about to fall apart. The American firm had licensed technology to the Japanese firm in exchange for cash and "best intention" to meet certain defined conditions. Several years later, it had become evident that the Japanese firm was not even close to meeting the conditions, and the American firm was threatening to terminate the relationship. The Japanese firms had also gotten irritated to the point where they were considering contesting the interpretation of this phrase in court.

The arrangement was poorly structured to begin with: "best intention" may be good enough between two Japanese firms, where other dealings can be used as leverage if conditions are not met, but such wording is usually not specific enough in individual relationships between Japanese and American firms. To keep the parties from going to court, I proposed a formula that would make the price for subsequent transfers of technology inversely proportional to the level of attainment of the conditions. The Japanese quickly accepted the concept and proceeded to negotiate the formula.

Perhaps the most elusive and challenging characteristic for which the global executive must strive is consistency. Consistency is usually derived from operating within a set of values that are not at odds with each other. When one is working between two cultures, having to understand perceptions and decisions in different and often contradictory contexts, one is forced to respond to each situation individually. The global executive can easily be caught in a no-win situation in which showing understanding for the Japanese position leads the American side to think that the executive has "gone Japanese." For example, turnover in an American organization sometimes inconveniences Japanese partners; yet some American managers feel that an apology is inappropriate because it would be a sign of weakness, particularly in the context of negotiations. I have had the stressful experience of negotiating a contract over several months only to have the U.S. company go through a change in policy just before the contract was signed, invalidating all the discussions and angering the Japanese, who had gone through the *ringi* ("consensus") process throughout their many levels of management.

Finally, the global executive requires mediation skills. Most negotiations between Japanese and Americans encounter impasses, either over substantive issues or because of cultural factors, when flexibility has been lost and neither side wishes to budge. In these cases, the global executive must make a judgment call, based on a knowledge of the two cultures and of the issues, on whether there is an intersection of the parties' "walkaway prices"—the point at which a party will walk away from the negotiating table. Pursuing deals that have no such intersection is clearly a waste of time; but in my experience, many eventually successful negotiations between firms from cultures as disparate as Japan and the United States tend to look initially as though there is no common ground.

The global executive who encounters such an impasse, but judges that there could be common ground, must work with both sides to get them to readjust their expectations. The parties may perceive this process negatively as compromising, but often a deal with compromised expectations is better than no deal at all. Needless to say, the global executive in this case requires much creativity and the ability to apply cross-cultural understanding, whether the negotiation is between Japanese and American partners, a firm and its foreign subsidiary, or a firm and its foreign customer.

WHY IS THERE A SHORTAGE OF TRULY GLOBAL EXECUTIVES?

It might seem puzzling that few people have the qualities just described. Hundreds of planes cross the oceans every day, and international telephone lines are overloaded. Why, then, are people not more tolerant of other people's values? One answer is that people tend not to stray from the precepts of their upbringing. Let us look first at the Japanese. Japanese executives boast about their world travels, yet when they travel, all their accommodations are arranged, an assistant travels with them, and wherever they go Japanese business associates meet them and compete to make their superiors comfortable. They work through translators and have little time to absorb foreign cultures. I firmly believe that until one has joked and argued with people from another country and engaged with them in their everyday activities, one has not really experienced that country but merely lived in an incubator.

I like to travel on my own, but recently, for the first time in my life, I took a Japanese packaged tour organized by my company. It taught me two things: what good service is supposed to mean (the Japanese travel agency did an excellent job) and how one can get by without interacting with a foreign culture. The reason such tours are popular is *anshinkan*: many Japanese are afraid of having to negotiate a cab fare or to enter a restaurant alone or to experience any other adventure that might be a source of trouble. Of course, this fear is not exclusive to the Japanese; many Americans take only packaged tours, and American expatriate employees in Japan often segregate themselves from the mainstream of Japanese society.

It would be nice to believe that Americans are less parochial, because the United States embraces many different cultures. In my decade and a half of living in the United States, however, when I traveled all over the country, I was amazed by the number of Americans who could not speak a second language, had never been out of their state, and had rigid ideas about how people should live. Although tight coupling and cohesion are not characteristic of the American culture, Americans seem to regard such values as individualism and freedom as absolute, perhaps out of pride in the power of America as a nation. My experience as a foreigner is that although Americans like to believe that anything goes in the United States, that is certainly not the case in the business world, where many taboos, preferred behavior patterns, and desirable images and traits thrive. Moreover, success and recognition in individual firms lead to the belief that what has worked against tremendous odds in the United States should be applicable anywhere in the world.

A survey done by Korn Ferry, a renowned executive search firm, compared American and non-American executives with respect to internationally related factors they considered important for the CEO of tomorrow. I was surprised by the following results:

	U.S. Executives	Non-U.S. Executives
Emphasizes international outlook	62%	82%
Experienced outside home country	35%	70%
Trained in a foreign language	19%	64%

The lack of foreign-language skills and foreign travel experience among U.S. executives tends to accentuate cultural distance and to create people who cannot face uncertainty and risk when operating in the international context. They cling to their native values, discounting the values of others, and tend to think of their own culture as somehow "right" or "normal"—the start of cultural prejudice. How many times I have heard tourists in a foreign country say of behavior that to them is unusual, "Normal people don't do that." The Japanese concept of *atarimae* ("intuitively obvious"), discussed in chapter 5, is a compilation of such "normal" Japanese behavior.

Consider the way Japanese-Americans and Americans in Japan are perceived. Having lived between the two cultures for a significant part of their lives, they tend to be the very people who have the best chance of understanding cross-cultural problems. Organizations should be developing them to play an important role in the international context. Yet these people tend to be looked on as minorities who are tangential to the community, and we collectively avoid taking advantage of this tremendous resource. A large number of Asian Americans work as engineers in Silicon Valley, but very few indeed work effectively at the interface between their culture of origin and the United States.

Many firms give training to develop a more global perspective in the minds of their managers and employees, but such training is often focused on the wrong areas. As we have seen, foreign-language instruction is important but not sufficient. Education in formalities such as bowing and giving and receiving business cards is useful, but it is not directly related to intercultural articulation and problem-solving ability. When Americans try to adapt to Japanese behavior by awkwardly bowing, the Japanese reaction beneath the polite expression is usually a frown. Most Japanese would agree that a little lapse in manners is easier to tolerate than the kind of poor intercultural articulation that leads to an impasse.

A more serious problem has to do with tight coupling on the Japanese side. Japanese who have gone abroad for their graduate schooling ought to become the ambassadors and leaders in orienting their organizations internationally. Yet, in a discussion with several Japanese alumni of a graduate school in the United States, when I asked whether after two years at the school they had had any adjustment problems when they returned to the Japanese employers who had sponsored them, the consensus was that they had not. The trick, they said, was to get through the schooling without being influenced by the American culture; that way, they would have the easiest re-entry into Japanese society. (I have seen this attitude reflected in the behavior of Japanese students in the United States, who often keep to themselves as a group, eating Japanese food, traveling together, speaking Japanese, and even preparing for exams together.) Moreover, the Japanese alumni told me, their Japanese employers were unlikely to give them any power to influence the operations of the business for at least five years. The purpose of their education in the United States, they felt, was more to understand American psychology and thought processes, which the firm was willing to incorporate into their strategy immediately on their return.

I was, quite frankly, amazed that these Japanese were so open with this information, and also angry that some Japanese firms are not using education abroad as a means not of internationalizing their organization but of obtaining prestigious degrees and an understanding of their competitors' mentality. If this thinking is widespread, it poses a serious issue for the American institutions training such students. In accepting them, the institutions are depriving American students of the chance to receive training and to turn it into useful experience.

Another problem in developing global executives is that after extensive training and experience, a person who indeed has the skills necessary to function effectively between two business cultures gets pigeonholed. Functions like a Japanese liaison office in American corporations are often looked on as service functions that are only peripheral to the actual running of the business. Anyone in this type of organization is in a no-win situation: the company wants to keep an effective employee in the same position; if performance is not good, the employee will not get anywhere either. Internationally oriented human resources need to develop their functional expertise through exposure to domestically oriented jobs. Pigeonholing deprives them of the chance to develop fully and integrate their international, functional, and managerial skills in order to work on high-leverage problems.

On the Japanese side, the problem is often more serious. Recently Japanese corporations have begun to hire foreigners not for their subsidiaries in foreign countries but for their companies in Japan. They have hailed this practice as a giant step forward in *kokusaika* ("internationalization"), and perhaps for the Japanese it is, but the foreigners hired are often placed in peripheral organizations or given work that is not fully integrated into the core of the organization. I will believe that the Japanese have turned international when they begin taking foreigners into the mainstream of their organizations, breaking through their tight coupling and their anxieties about heterogeneity.

Kenichi Takemura, a noted social critic in Japan, once interviewed the president of the Kansai Airport Corporation. They discussed how good the Americans are at large projects such as designing airports and the communities surrounding airports, and the president indicated that American companies had been consulted on the airport planned for Osaka. When Takemura asked, "Instead of asking for their recommendations, why not give them a contract and have them do it?" there was no clear answer. Having the Americans build the airport would bring foreigners into the core of the project and introduce heterogeneity, which risks breaking the delicate interdependence within the organization and between the organization and other stakeholders, such as financial institutions and Japanese subcontractors.

This approach is not surprising, because the Japanese differentiate with respect to their own people. For example, a large Japanese electronics house might establish a quota for the new college graduates who will be assigned to each of its divisions. Suppose that one division wants more. One option it has is to create or take a subsidiary company—say, a company that does software development for the parent corporation—and hire people into that organization. Usually the division is ahead of the game in its timing and thus gets the better people. This is one method of differentiating working conditions, pay, and other benefits without creating heterogeneity in the division's human resources policies. For example, if it is deemed that flex time is good for software development, the division may implement it in the subsidiary but not in the division itself.

A Harvard Business School student asked the president of Mitsubishi International Corporation (Mitsubishi's American subsidiary) when he might expect to see an American running MIC. Again, there was no clear answer. As I mentioned earlier in the book, the presidency of MIC has been one of the paths leading to the presidency of the parent corporation. This is one way in which the parent corporation can wield control over the subsidiary and at the same time place someone it is comfortable with to run the subsidiary located in the country that is perhaps its most important trading partner.

DEVELOPING GLOBALIZED EMPLOYEES

Companies that take their global activities seriously invest significantly in the development of their international human resources. Several approaches are used in an effort to instill in their human resources the extensive knowledge and skills needed to be effective in the international context.

Training Programs

Many firms known for their international activities provide extensive training to employees who participate in international business. Basic training begins with a study of the country with which one needs to become familiar. The culture of the country, including its values, norms, and rituals, is important and should be considered separately from social basics such as religion, protocol, features of the language, and other niceties somewhat removed from direct applicability to business. A solid understanding of the economy and business environment and of the state of international relations is also needed.

Unfortunately, many companies stop at the theoretical level. Cultural understanding alone is not enough; one must know how to apply those concepts in such crucial business situations as starting and maintaining cross-cultural relationships, decision making, motivation, conflict resolution, articulation, interactive communication, negotiation, persuasion, and presentation skills. Interactive communication is not a trivial endeavor for the Japanese, because there is no natural mechanism in the Japanese language to confirm the details of a prior conversation; one is supposed to infer it (*satori*). Thus, something as seemingly simple as a presentation poses problems, even when it involves the same overhead projector and the same English language. In an American presentation, the audience is usually free to ask questions as the presentation progresses and the initiative for understanding is taken by the listeners. Often the objectives and conclusions of the presentations are stated up front in order to orient the audience. In a Japanese presentation, the speaker takes the initiative in promoting understanding among the listeners, by anticipating questions and incorporating them into the presentation. Thus, usually no questions are asked until the speaker finishes presenting. And contextual information is presented first, with the conclusion usually coming at the end. It is understandable that this set-up tends to make an American listener impatient. Such interactive skills are usually acquired not through lectures but through role plays, cases, and exercises.

Functional skills must also be taught. The extensive curriculum of one Japanese firm includes the following:

- Trade: The basics of import and export
- Advertising and selling in a foreign land
- Standards and safety regulations in foreign countries
- International contracts
- Foreign exchange
- Labor management in a cross-cultural context
- Legal aspects of foreign business (including education on dumping, antitrust, using a lawyer, and personnel regulations)
- Insurance

The American firm trying to educate its people on how to do business in Japan can do something analogous, but runs into one obstacle: finding the appropriate instructors.

The problem is the difficulty of knowing who are the real "Japan experts." Some American executives spend one week in Japan, call themselves literate on Japan, and teach "Japan courses." Peer pressure for American executives to be assertive and look informed often encourages this kind of misrepresentation, but it is extremely dangerous.

There are many outside "Japan experts" willing to market their services. Some have a superficial understanding of Japan but excellent presentation skills and a logical set of arguments that a person who has done business in Japan can spot as being off the mark. Others are knowledgeable about Japan but Americanize their descriptions of Japanese business practices to the point where the American students end up thinking they understand more than they actually do. I once heard an American professor describe a supplier-customer relationship in Japan as akin to a *shitauke* ("subcontractor") relationship. Not only is this incorrect, but one student remembered the concept as *shiitake,* as in Japanese mushrooms. Imagine the impression he would make if he mistakenly used that word in front of a Japanese executive.

A comprehensive training program targets all the employees in the firm who are concerned with U.S.-Japanese business. Several types of employees fit this description: Americans working in Japan, Japanese working in the United States, and people at both ends who support the first two groups. NEC, for example, provides the following training for Japanese employees who are to be stationed in the United States:

- English language
- Basics of trade

- NEC product line overview
- Overseas marketing
- Finance and foreign exchange
- Legal aspects
- Insurance
- Personnel policies
- Accounting

The objective of this program clearly is to prepare the Japanese employee to become functional in the United States. A different objective drives the training intended for American managers working in NEC's overseas locations. The following set of courses makes clear that the aim is not only to enhance people's understanding of Japan but to make them "NEC men and women."

- The Japanese economy and its future
- Japanese management
- Japanese culture
- International management
- Japanese labor policies
- The internationalization of NEC
- C&C (computers and communications—NEC's corporate mission)
- Overview of NEC's product lines
- NEC's personnel policies
- Quality control

It is clear that NEC is trying to establish a common set of values across its global organization.

Of course, nothing in training works as effectively as actual experience. Unfortunately, many programs end at the conceptual level and stop short of skill acquisition. On-the-job training in the form of temporary assignments overseas or, even more simply, participation in meetings that involve foreign businesspeople, is an excellent means of learning.

Visits and Exchanges

Cultural familiarity is really a function of the duration and intensity of cross-cultural experience, usually in a foreign country. If Japan is an important market to an American firm, it is particularly important that senior executives make visits to Japan on a regular basis, not only to work out sales opportunities and relationship issues but also to understand, support, and develop the local personnel in the Japanese subsidiary. Many executives do this on the surface, but the challenge is what happens after the visit. In order to develop one's international perspective in a dynamic fashion, one must follow up on the issues raised in a visit to Japan. It is all too easy for even the most thorough American executive to fail to do so—owing to distance, the time difference, and the tendency of the Japanese to keep quiet. Without follow-up, however, a visit yields only static, snapshot views of business in Japan that by themselves are worth little.

I am a believer in rotational programs, despite all the problems I have seen with them. Two key issues require attention. First, given the expense and opportunity costs of such an exchange, learning in the foreign culture must be maximized. That should be obvious, but it does not always happen; we have already seen how both expatriate

Americans and expatriate Japanese tend to isolate themselves from the foreign environment. Moreover, the organization accepting foreign personnel must aggressively try to engage them in business discussions: observer status is not enough.

In the case of partnerships, it is even better to rotate personnel into a Japanese partner's organization if the competitive situation permits. Toshiba and Hewlett Packard effected such an exchange of personnel in the area of semiconductors. These intensive immersion experiences do the most for behavior modification.

The second issue that must be faced regarding rotation is repatriation. These exchanges represent sizable investments for the firms involved; and if people are not successfully repatriated back to their original organizations, there is a risk of losing them. Needless to say, that defeats the whole purpose.

Japanese firms, as we have seen, practically order their people to relocate to overseas subsidiaries. In return, they usually also take responsibility for the re-entry of transferred employees into the Japanese organization. They assign to headquarters "godfathers," perhaps with overseas experience, who discuss various personal issues with the employee, including transferring back. NEC's "re-entry boss" scheme is a good example of this kind of plan.

Some American firms do a bad job of handling re-entry. Transfer personnel become a target of the pigeonholing phenomenon described earlier in the chapter and have a difficult time finding a re-entry path. Those firms that practice career planning can provide some help; but those that rely on a free-market, "jobs-are-up-for-grabs" style of placement end up with poor return yields. In a country like Japan, exchanges are so costly that one can ill afford to lose the contributions of exchange personnel back at headquarters. Even if all such personnel re-entered successfully, there would still be room for improvement in understanding and supporting the effort to penetrate the Japanese market.

I once heard that one hundred times as many Japanese businesspeople are stationed in the United States as there are American businesspeople in Japan. From the considerable time I have spent in both Japan and the United States, I would venture to say that the Japanese business environment is much harder to comprehend than the American. A large part of this difficulty, as we saw earlier, stems from the tendency of the Japanese not to give feedback. As a result, more people are needed to go from the United States to Japan to study, plan, and strategize than are needed in the opposite direction. Otherwise, the Japanese will continue to claim that Americans do not deserve to penetrate Japan because they are not genuinely trying.

Targeting the Younger Generation

Although wisdom comes with age, the older one gets the more one becomes comfortable with one's own values, and those values tend to solidify. The young are still impressionable and can adapt to the international environment within a relatively short period of time. For some time, the Japanese have talked about the *shinjinrui* ("the new breed"), workers under the age of twenty-five who represent a new attitude toward work. A leading Japanese newspaper described their characteristics as follows:

- They have a clear and articulated preference for a higher-paying job.
- They ascribe a high importance to working enjoyably with colleagues.
- They are dissatisfied with the current Japanese company structure, work system, and philosophy. They don't want to take work home, hate to sacrifice their personal life for work, dislike people whose sole life is work, and are not satisfied with current labor practices.
- They have a preference for a specialist rather than a generalist (management/administration) career.
- They have an affinity for information and high technology.

This description is not consistent with the tight coupling in Japanese business described elsewhere in this book. Most Japanese managers in their forties and fifties tell me that they do not know how to deal with this generation.

One barrier to the *shinjinrui*'s being able to create change in the Japanese organization is the marked differentiation the Japanese make between being a child and being a *shakaijin* ("responsible adult and member of society"). Companies often take advantage of this distinction to train young people to forget their "distorted" past ideologies and conform to the status quo. Despite this effort, the young generation in Japanese companies is persisting in holding different attitudes, ones that tend to be much more open and adventurous than those of their elders—more in line with internationally oriented people. They are less inhibited about expressing their opinions and state their thoughts with a clarity that bothers many senior people.

The Japanese should make use of this tendency, instead of trying to suppress it, and channel these basic values into efforts to develop a more international environment in the firm. Tolerating heterogeneous thinking when a Japanese employee comes back from two years of schooling in the United States would be a good start.

Some Japanese firms have made the leap of faith and are investing in the young. Honda is already known as a company of youthful thinking. Bridgestone, the tire manufacturer, plunges new employees into English-language training immediately after they start work and provides the opportunity for short-term overseas study in a U.S. university early in their careers.

American firms should involve young American employees in as many cross-cultural business discussions and negotiations as possible, to prevent their biases from being crystallized. They should also send relatively young people on overseas assignments, particularly to Japan. Local Japanese employees tend to be much less defensive about relatively young transferees. That fact, combined with the adventurousness that comes with being young, enhances the chances that the transferred employee will understand the interactions behind the scene.

. . .

Two conditions are essential to the success of the efforts just described. The first is a supportive environment that encourages people to be internationally minded. Such an environment has to start with senior executives who value international activities and the skills of their international human resources. Management interest in penetrating the Japanese market must be backed up by a commitment to support the people lower in the organization and related to the firm's Japanese business; otherwise, these people will at best be hampered by the rest of the organization. This commitment must include following through on promises to Japanese customers and distributors, providing continuity despite organizational changes, developing careers for global executives, and being flexible about standard operating procedure.

When one is dealing with a distant culture like that of Japan, this support becomes critical. Often I see American executives who have little time to listen to the people who are close to the firm's Japanese business, and who instead are quick to show discouragement and disapproval based on preconceived notions and biases. Under these circumstances, international people are bound to lose their motivation. Business problems, even those that relate to the American market, tend to be complex; and one cannot expect Japanese people to discuss their problems in English with the same efficiency and logical persuasion as American managers do about American matters. One should open one's mind and be brave enough to explore ideas that may not seem reasonable at first.

The second prerequisite is an open value system. Given the problems of bias and pigeonholing described earlier, it is important that top executives in a firm decree a set of values that discourage bias, and that they act as role models in applying those values. The most important goal in doing so would be to provide the internationally oriented people with a degree of freedom in problem solving and mobility within the organization. The firm's effectiveness in the international arena would thereby be maximized, because hybrid people could be utilized for important cross-cultural tasks with a minimum of bias. Good international human resources would not be pigeonholed and could continue to develop their managerial and functional capabilities and grow with the organization.

Developing the global executive is an uphill battle. It involves a change of behavior, and the path from an intellectual understanding of a different culture to the ability to apply that knowledge is long. Often it requires extensive deconditioning of innate values and behavior patterns. That is why companies like NEC not only invest in cross-cultural training programs but also have developed an overall international human resource policy designed to motivate the employee assigned to go abroad.

First, NEC selects carefully its overseas assignees, looking for such qualities as initiative, vitality, curiosity, and leadership skills. Of course, aptitude in a foreign language and previous experience overseas are considered to be pluses. On the personal side, health and family situation are taken into consideration.

Not only is extensive training planned, but there is an attempt to plan the overseas rotation. At the same time, the re-entry boss scheme, mentioned earlier, assures that someone back at Japanese headquarters is available to respond to professional and personal difficulties and to take the responsibility for a smooth re-entry onto the Japanese corporate ladder.

Compensation of overseas assignees is based on assuring a reasonable standard of living while maintaining equity with others in the firm, as is generally true of American firms. NEC also arranges for language and cultural training for the spouses of the employees transferred; and once a year, a Japanese doctor is sent around the foreign locations to check on the medical status of the families stationed abroad.

It should be evident that development of effective global executives requires planning. Such human resources seldom materialize from a free-market, "learn-what-you-can-from-on-the-job-training" approach. Whether a firm has the discipline to develop and accommodate them will in the medium to long term determine its global competitiveness.

7

Cross-Cultural Partnerships

I HAVE LOOKED at some of the difficulties and tradeoffs involved in conducting business in a cross-cultural environment. In the case of American firms seeking to penetrate the Japanese market, I considered three phases, from initial entry to becoming a semi-insider, largely in the context of the American firm operating independently. Partnering is an alternative that can help significantly in accomplishing these same objectives.

In recent years, partnerships have come first into vogue and then under criticism. A number of books and articles have advocated partnerships as a way of gaining global leadership in industries where worldwide coverage would be difficult for any single firm. Others, however, have criticized partnering, particularly with the Japanese, as a one-way street on which important know-how flows from Western partners to the Japanese. And certainly many American executives I know are highly skeptical of any Japanese partnership arrangements that involve intellectual property.

Thus, while partnering is strategically desirable in improving QCDS capability and in attaining semi-insider status in Japan, execution of such partnership arrangements is a test of one's ability to deal in a cross-cultural setting. I shall, in the first part of this chapter, deal with the local and global motives for partnering and the various tradeoffs involved and, in later sections, discuss some of the problems firms encounter in cross-cultural partnering and consider how to increase the chances of success through the partnership route.

LOCAL MOTIVES FOR PARTNERING

Entering the Japanese Market: Go It Alone or Join Hands?

There is much debate about whether an American firm should enter the Japanese market by establishing a wholly owned subsidiary in Japan or by going into a joint venture. In some industries, the Japanese government historically gave foreign firms no choice but to partner, as a means of inducing technology infusion. By contrast, most Japanese firms entering the United States market have formed wholly owned subsidiaries, for two reasons. First, when Japanese firms entered the American market several decades ago, they had little technology to barter and, in fact, wanted to obtain technology from the Americans. Second, the American government did not require foreign firms that wished to participate in the U.S. market to partner and to provide benefits in some form to American firms and investors.

American firms now entering the Japanese market have a greater choice between setting up a wholly owned subsidiary and entering a joint venture. Joint ventures with a Japanese firm can help foreign firms accelerate the process of gaining *anshinkan* and becoming semi-insiders in the Japanese business environment in a number of ways. The involvement of a credible Japanese partner contributes immensely to the reputation of the enterprise and can make a difference in anything from finding office space in a choice location to securing financing. The use of manufacturing or other capabilities of the Japanese partner can improve QCDS—the combination of quality, cost, delivery, and service described in the first four chapters—and offer the Japanese customer *anshinkan* in the form of more local content in the product. Management involvement by the Japanese partner can also raise the level of sensitivity to Japanese expectations regarding QCDS.

A partnership can help the foreign firm to become a semi-insider in Japan in several ways. First, the Japanese firm can contribute human resources, although given the permanent employment system it is prudent to make sure that the joint venture does not become a dumping ground for employees with poor performance. Second, Japanese backing and connections can show confidence in the American firm and be instrumental in supporting relationships with key customers, distributors, and the government. Finally, Japanese management involvement tends to temper and make palatable American decision making in the Japanese business environment.

Fuji Xerox is a successful joint venture in which many of these advantages can be seen. The partnership allowed Fuji Film to diversify into the area of photocopying, and ultimately allowed Xerox and Rank Xerox, its British subsidiary, to penetrate Japan and establish a base of operations there. The Kobayashi father-son combination provided significant guidance, not only in terms of leadership of the joint venture but through constant interaction with the Western partner to keep the two parties in harmony.

Not all firms value the joint venture as an entry vehicle. Some firms, such as AMP (an American supplier of electrical connectors), will enter international markets only through a wholly owned subsidiary, and if a government restricts that form of investment, the company simply waits to enter that market until the restrictions are lifted. Let me look, then, at the tradeoffs between the wholly owned subsidiary and the joint venture as a form of entry into an international marketplace.

The advantages of the wholly owned subsidiary relate mainly to comfort and control. In comparison with a joint venture, a subsidiary can operate with a set of cultural values closer to that of headquarters. It encounters fewer marketing problems relating to antitrust laws and therefore has more direct control of decisions regarding pricing and distribution channels. Because the company has total equity control, no restrictions result from the partner's own agenda. Finally, communications and transfer of technology can take place quite openly, without the precautions that would have to be taken in a joint venture.

The disadvantage of working through a wholly owned subsidiary is that one must start out from scratch as an outsider. No Japanese partner is committed to the endeavor to give advice on operating in the Japanese business environment or to help procure the necessary human resources. Finally, the entire start-up is done at the company's own risk.

The joint venture has a number of advantages. It provides access to the partner's strengths, although this access must be negotiated. The investment, whether of money or of human resources, is shared; therefore, the risk is usually shared. Although dealing with the partner is not always easy, one also receives much guidance on the implications of specific business decisions in the Japanese business environment. This guidance can be important in a culture as distant as Japan's.

On the negative side are the factors mentioned earlier, such as less flexibility in overall strategic direction and in particular in marketing decisions because of antitrust limitations. In addition, the valuation of contributions made by each partner tends to be a sensitive issue. Problems can arise whenever an incremental contribution is made, not just on start-up of the joint venture.

The roster of the highest earners among foreign companies in Japan reveals no correlation between success and the choice of one or the other of these forms. It includes both wholly owned subsidiaries like IBM Japan and joint ventures like Fuji Xerox. The key to success is rather that in each case the parent firm considered which form would be more advantageous given its own situation, and worked to maximize the advantages of the chosen structure and to minimize its limitations. I explore this subject in more detail later in the chapter.

Using a Partnership to Build Strengths

Many American firms that enter Japan by establishing a wholly owned subsidiary find that as the subsidiary grows, partnering is a good method of developing its capabilities. Such subsequent partnerships, designed to provide further *anshinkan* or further penetration into the tightly coupled Japanese business environment or both, can be either close relationships such as joint ventures or arm's-length cooperative efforts in which no additional legal entity is set up. The types of partnerships in this category are limited only by the creativity of the human mind. I shall look at just three kinds of arrangements.

Contract Manufacturing for Local Demand

The Japanese often like to visit the plant at which their products are manufactured. One way for products to be manufactured locally without a huge manufacturing investment involves using the excess capacity of a Japanese manufacturer of a similar product on a contract manufacturing basis. One can often use such arrangements to come closer to meeting the QCDS expectations of the Japanese customer. There are, however, at least two factors one must consider in order to secure a constant supply of product at the right terms and on a continuing basis. The first has to do with the contractor's motives and capacity conditions. The second involves the tradeoffs in deciding whether to use the contracted capacity for local demand or for worldwide demand. I discuss both of these factors later in this chapter.

Joint Product Development

Also, as I have said, Japanese customers expect products and services to be tailored to their own wants, not sold in standard formats. For example, cookie manufacturers in Japan wrap each cookie separately, and each manufacturer has a different wrapping style that those who supply the wrapping must accommodate. In order to compete effectively in such an environment, one must fully understand the diverse needs of various customers and manufacture products in line with those complexities.

Tailoring the product of an American manufacturer to the needs of a Japanese customer or group of customers requires that the customer divulge some knowhow. Often customers are unwilling to do so, however, especially to an entity they have not dealt with and therefore do not trust. It therefore makes sense for an American firm that wants to do such product tailoring to partner with a Japanese firm that already has access to customers and complementary technology.

On the other hand, this type of arrangement tests the ability of the American firm to break into a relationship between two Japanese firms. The Americans must make a conscientious and persistent effort to remain involved with the customer; given the cohesiveness of the Japanese, it is all too easy for the foreign firm to slip into the limited role of provider of technology and development knowhow and to become isolated from the customer. The Japanese, intentionally or unintentionally, let this happen, because of the risk that the Americans might act out of line and jeopardize their long relationship with the customer.

189

For the Japanese, the customer relationship is as valuable an intangible asset as the product or service know-how of the American firm. Ultimately, these arrangements are tested when the parties decide who is going to supply the product to the Japanese customers.

Cooperation in Marketing and Distribution

In the United States, a manufacturer often tries to find independent (or at least relatively independent) distributors to carry its products. In Japan, by contrast, setting up one's own distribution channels takes an enormous amount of time. In the tightly coupled Japanese business environment, good distributors in any product category will tend to have strong affiliations, and many of these distributors would not easily risk jeopardizing such relationships in order to take on a new product from a supplier in the United States.

One way to work around this barrier is to cooperate with a Japanese manufacturer who has a complementary product line, and use that firm's channels. For example, it would be impossible for any individual retailer of, say, Mitsubishi Motors to make an independent decision to carry an import; but if Mitsubishi Motors comes to an agreement with an American automobile manufacturer to do so, all the retailers would feel *anshinkan* in carrying the product.

There are, however, some challenges to this type of arrangement, beginning with the terms and conditions regarding margin and supply guarantees. The latter factor is usually sensitive, because if the American supplier cannot meet Japanese expectations for QCDS, the Japanese partner will be caught between the Japanese customer and the American firm's ability to supply a dependable product. Beyond that, however, there is the channel conflict I described in chapter 2: if the American manufacturer already has a channel of its own in Japan, would a cooperative arrangement lead to confusion? Differences in interpretation of antitrust laws tend to lead to problems. As mentioned earlier, in Japan, when two retailers or distributors get into what the Japanese call a "batting" situation in which they compete for business from the same customer, the manufacturer usually steps in with *shidoh* ("guidance") to arbitrate. This practice is patently illegal according to the American interpretation of antitrust laws; and in Japan, it is also superficially illegal unless territorial coverage is specifically defined in the franchise agreement.

Americans also become uncomfortable when Japanese distributors carry competing lines. Japanese trading companies generally have multiple divisions and subsidiary firms to which they can parcel out the lines of competing American suppliers, another example of what they call "competition and cooperation." To American manufacturers, who expect loyalty and commitment from distributors, this is not a happy situation.

. . .

Despite these challenges, if an American firm negotiates reasonable terms it can live with, and commits itself to making the arrangement work, partnering can significantly enhance its capability locally in Japan. Let me now examine how partnering can be used to further an American firm's global strategies.

GLOBAL MOTIVES FOR PARTNERING

One reason partnering became such a popular concept is that it can be used as an integral part of a firm's worldwide strategy. Industries, particularly those that are capital-intensive, are becoming more global as they try to amortize their high up-front fixed costs over as many units as possible. That means participating in as many markets around the world as they can; those who deal in limited market-places may lose the cost battle. In the semiconductor industry, for example, manufacturers who aggressively sold manufacturing-intensive dynamic RAMs around the world in volume reaped enormous cost advantages over those who did not. This motive for partnering could mean sharing investment costs as well as marketing cooperation in different parts of the world.

Another motive for partnering lies in the exponential growth of product variations as customers demand more choice in their purchasing decisions. In the automotive business, customers are demanding more body styles, more options, and more price points. In the semiconductor industry, customers are demanding more customized functions and more types of packaging. In many such businesses, it is becoming impossible for a single manufacturer to develop and produce a product line of the size needed to compete. This challenge is compounded as the market comes to expect shorter and shorter lead times for product development. Since many electronic products have product life cycles of no more than six months, manufacturers are forced to overlap development phases in order to keep pace. In these situations, partnerships can divide the labor among several manufacturers so that all the partners end up with a bigger product line than they would have on an individual basis. For example, Toshiba partnered with General Electric and Siemens in the area of application-specific integrated circuits, and the three firms divided the work of creating a library that all parties could integrate and sell.

Different manufacturers in different parts of the world often have the various functional strengths needed to manage a particular product line. For example, an American producer might excel at product definition and development and a Japanese producer at manufacturing. Or, within a single function such as manufacturing, an American firm might excel at producing a high-end product whereas a Japanese firm is better at producing low-end products. One reason for aggressive partnering and sharing is that companies often find that they need a certain skill set earlier than they can develop it themselves. Their only recourse is to obtain it from another company; and short of a straight acquisition, some form of partnership is often the answer.

Yet another motive for partnership lies in intellectual property rights. Intellectual property laws foster creativity by protecting the innovators but, at the same time, reinforce the territoriality of technical know-how. If a firm holds a patent on a particular manufacturing process, no one can even accidentally stumble on that method without being accused of infringement. Planning new products and diversification, therefore, almost always requires thorough investigation of the intellectual property rights involved and a licensing or cross-licensing of those rights.

THE TRADEOFF BETWEEN LOCAL AND
GLOBAL MOTIVES FOR PARTNERING

Resources, whether human, capital, or material, are scarce in almost every firm worldwide, and this limitation also drives a tradeoff in the area of partnering. For example, although Japanese interest in a potential partnership with an American firm could span distribution channels or overseas manufacturing capacity, Japanese firms are often interested in intellectual rights held by American firms. In such cases, the American firm must consider carefully whether to trade the intellectual property for help in penetrating the Japanese market or to use it to increase the firm's worldwide competitiveness.

Another potential area of tradeoff is subcontracting. If an American firm subcontracts manufacturing of a product line to a Japanese firm, it must decide how much of that supply will be used for the local Japanese market and how much for meeting worldwide demand. If the firm can realize a higher price for the product in non-Japanese markets, then allocating any portion of the subcontracted supply to Japan would mean that the American parent feels that it is in its long-term strategic interests to penetrate the market.

Whenever a firm must decide how much of its partnering will address local needs and how much global needs, it will make the right tradeoff if penetrating the Japanese market is positioned in the context of gaining worldwide competitiveness in the long term. The short-term nature of American financial and managerial systems, however, makes this positioning a challenge.

PICKING THE RIGHT PARTNER

Regardless of the structure of a projected partnership, partners must be compatible. Several elements must be considered in making this crucial choice.

First, partners should be culturally compatible and willing to adjust. When the two firms share values, perhaps because they are in the same business and have to respond to the same pressures, their relationship is likely to progress smoothly. As in a marriage, when one side is too rigid, difficulties arise. Firms that have a strong culture have to find adjustment mechanisms if the partner relationship is to be a good one.

Second, the firms' motive should align. It is important for both partners to understand the other's motives for entering into the relationship. In reality, however, the stated motive for a partnership is often inconsistent with the hidden agenda. This discrepancy creates a dangerous situation, particularly if a long-term partnership is projected; at some point there will be a strategic divergence. It may be better to accept this disagreement and agree that the arrangement will be temporary.

Third, the partners should have complementary sets of skills. Professor William Davidson of the University of Southern California believes that firms with similar skills work better together, because a firm generally prefers not to be totally dependent on the skills of its partner. In my own experience, complementary sets of skills tend to be an important element in holding the partnership together.

Fourth, the partners must be eager to improve their position or diversify. Japanese firms, used to tight coupling, often do not allow an American firm access to their capabilities in an area in which they are strong unless they desperately need something from the American firm. In many cases, the Japanese firm wishes to diversify into a new product line or market, and if an American firm possesses something valuable, a trade may be arranged in which the Japanese firm helps the American firm penetrate the Japanese market.

Finally, reputation helps in Japan, as does being honorable.

NEGOTIATING THE QUID PRO QUO

Negotiations between a Japanese firm and an American firm are never easy, even when their objectives are compatible. Not only are the actual contract terms and conditions hard to agree on, but the process is often full of misunderstanding and emotional ups and downs.

Historically, the Japanese government restricted foreign equity participation in the Japanese market unless technology was transferred in some manner to a Japanese firm. For a developing nation this policy made sense. It induced the infusion of technology and prevented foreign firms from simply reaping returns from the Japanese market without contributing to the Japanese economy and to Japanese businesses. Most foreign firms had to abide by these restrictions; a well-known exception is Texas Instruments (TI), which refused to license the Japanese unless it could set up a wholly owned subsidiary in Japan. Sony served as a temporary partner to satisfy this need; and after several years, TI bought back the shares.

Today the Japanese have money and can make attractive offers for technology and brands. In most circumstances they are willing to pay significant cash up front in return for unlimited rights to technology. Cash is abundant; and for the Japanese, an outright purchase is cheaper in the long run than allowing American firms an entrée into their tightly coupled network of relationships or their know-how. Moreover, the Japanese are accustomed to using foreign ideas freely, and often everyone in the Japanese business environment demands that type of flexibility. I once asked a Japanese firm to write down the terms that they and their distribution channels could live with. What came back was unlimited copying rights, unlimited derivative and modification rights, no approval or tracking responsibilities, the ability to pass through rights—in short, a virtual carte blanche.

This phenomenon is partially explained by the unique method by which the Japanese absorb know-how. The insular nature of Japan has contributed to the Japanese ability to shield itself from foreign ideas and values being forced upon them. As a result, the Japanese have perhaps had the most freedom in the world to adapt foreign know-how to their own situation. Taichi Sakaiya calls this *eetokotori,* or "taking just the good parts." The Japanese have been able to absorb foreign know-how without its underlying thought process and cultural values, and thus have maintained intact their principal values: hence, the bafflement of a foreign tourist in Tokyo at seeing everywhere signs containing a concatenation of English words that is incomprehensible to the westerner.

Complicating negotiations even further is the fact that until recently the Japanese have had a lax notion of intellectual property. The idea of an individual or a special group receiving windfall returns just for developing a useful technology goes counter to the group-oriented behavior of the Japanese, particularly their sharing of profit and pain. The Japanese attitude is now changing, because the Western world is taking intellectual property seriously and because Japan's own intellectual property is being infringed on by less-developed nations.

American firms, however, are often willing to license non–state-of-the-art technology for a price and acceptable terms and conditions under which the intellectual property will be used. Although the Japanese motive in paying hefty sums up front is to minimize royalties, which would become variable costs for them, American firms accept cash up front only to maximize profit dollars and to make the quarter's financial statements look good. Abegglen, the author of Kaisha (1985), claims that this shortsightedness of American firms has permitted Japanese firms to pick up the results of close to twenty years of technology development for a fraction of what the United States is spending on research and development in a single year. Moreover, by accepting cash, the American firms give up their largest leverage for gaining access to the tightly coupled Japanese business environment.

As we have seen, two other types of partnership involve distribution and subcontracting. I noted that Japanese firms are not usually willing to offer market access to American firms in a partnership arrangement unless they need something desperately. Most successful market-access arrangements have occurred when the Japanese firm wanted to enter the product category the American firm was strong in, and planned to build a distribution channel with the

American firm. For the Americans, this requires taking the time to develop a distribution channel rather than picking up a ready-made channel; but if the Japanese partner has strong distribution channels in another product line, that experience can be useful.

In the area of subcontracting, a different set of challenges awaits the negotiator. I have seen two types of subcontracting involving an American firm and a Japanese contractor in a variety of industries. In the first, a dedicated subcontractor does work purely on an economic basis. The price paid per unit by the American firm provides enough return to the Japanese firm, even after the fixed-cost investment put out by the Japanese subcontractor is taken into account. Such arrangements, however, do not constitute the majority of subcontracting deals. The second, more common type of subcontractor is a manufacturer who markets products under the firm's own label and performs contracting only if it has excess capacity or if there is some strategic reason outweighing the cost of diverting capacity that could be used to manufacture products with higher value added. Given the same capacity, producing its own products brings the Japanese manufacturer higher revenue and a stabler base of demand. For example—although this is a case of an American firm subcontracting for a Japanese firm—Nikkei Sangyo reported on 28 June 1989 that Schmide Machine and Tools revoked a subcontracting arrangement with Mitsubishi Heavy Industries in which Schmide was to manufacture machine tools for MHI for the U.S. market; the stated reason for the cancellation was a dramatic upturn in Schmide's own orders. It is therefore a challenge for an American firm to manage a contracting arrangement so as to be able to depend on a stable source of supply. Managing the opposite end is also difficult: when demand for the product goes down, the subcontractor suffers, and motivation wanes.

SIGNING IS ONLY HALF THE VICTORY: CHALLENGES TO IMPLEMENTATION

Few partnerships work out as originally planned. For example, many partnerships that are conceived as semipermanent go through their active life in a few years; in those cases, the American partner sometimes ends up with the short end of the stick. The experience of Honeywell in Japan is illustrative. In the 1960s, Honeywell licensed computer technology to NEC. It also set up a Japanese subsidiary, but for a variety of reasons, depending on whom one asks—a change in corporate strategies, not having the appropriate product line for the Japanese market, and so on—Honeywell decided to terminate its activities in that product line in Japan and sell the shares of its Japanese subsidiary to NEC. Despite the fact that Honeywell has a successful operation in Japan in a different product line, in the form of a joint venture with Yamatake, such effective divestitures after the transfer of technology are a cause for distrust in partnering endeavors between the two countries.

Competitive Aspects of Partnerships

Although partnerships are supposed to be cooperative, often they are formed by two or more competitors. In teaching a course on partnering to high-level executives of Western firms in Japan, I was amazed at the number of times I was asked how to keep one's Japanese partner from walking away with one's know-how. There is some merit to this concern. Taichi Sakaiya claims that throughout Japanese history, the longest time it has ever taken Japan to "one-up" the foreign source from which it gained the know-how is forty years. He cites various examples, including not only recent industrial products but also Buddhist statues (cast-type) and guns from several centuries ago. Indeed, many Western firms have lost significant value in partnerships with the Japanese, but I am not sure that the Japanese are totally at fault.

The technology and know-how leakages that frequently cause disagreements often result from problems in implementation. When a technology transfer engineer is assigned to effect the transfer of a certain type of technology, the engineer does not always have a copy of the agreement stipulating the limits of the technology to be transferred. Particularly in a subcontracting situation, where the transfer engineer might be evaluated on how quickly the subcontractor can begin production, much related know-how that was not intended to be passed on can be released. American firms must be careful to limit the scope of the transfer so that the most strategic pieces of technology do not leak out. One way to do this is to limit technology partnerships to mature products.

In the other direction, the tight coupling of Japanese organizations, together with the low turnover rate, tends to lead to much less leakage. At the same time, American firms miss many opportunities to benefit from the know-how of their Japanese partners. The reason seems to be largely cultural. Learning ability is dependent on one's receptivity to other ideas and on one's astuteness in seeing ways to apply these ideas to one's own situation. Because of their emphasis on individualism and freedom of opinion, Americans have a not-invented-here attitude that serves as a major barrier to the infusion of know-how from the Japanese. I recall an American manufacturing manager who, after visiting a Japanese competitor's plant that clearly had better productivity indicators, concluded that because of cultural and management differences the visit was only of surface interest. In reporting the visit, he made his factory seem just as good as the Japanese plant, for fear that management would think he was doing a poor job at home.

By contrast, the stereotypical image of Japanese taking dozens of pictures of foreign technology suggests the aggressiveness with which they bring these bits of know-how back to their firms. They assume that there is always room for improvement, and look for any hints they can get from what others are doing.

A related cause of asymmetry in transfer of know-how is the American emphasis on learning for oneself. For many American managers, it is not enough to hear about another manager's visit to a Japanese plant; they can learn only from their own experience. Meanwhile, the Japanese not only send droves of people to the United States but circulate their reports widely and study the reports to the point where they almost make another's experience their own.

One arrangement I have seen recently that is of interest here is the case of an American company trading a stream of product licenses for participation in a manufacturing joint venture with the Japanese licensee. The Japanese firm gets a license on the next generation of products only if the joint venture plant meets certain operational goals. If the relationship can be maintained, this sort of set-up may be extremely valuable for the American firm, since it allows manufacturing know-how to be transferred to the American firm in a dynamic manner which in turn allows the American firm to replicate the manufacturing know-how. A manufacturing joint venture is probably one of the few effective ways to pick up manufacturing know-how from the Japanese.

Of course, whether this arrangement can last for a long time is another question altogether. Clearly, each partner will race toward self-sufficiency; and when one side doesn't need the other anymore, the other's negotiating position will weaken. But even if temporary, both parties could derive much value from this type of arrangement.

Protecting Intellectual Property

The United States and Japan have fundamentally different views on intellectual property. Americans value the pioneering spirit highly, and one way to encourage it is to protect people's ideas. Developers of intellectual property can obtain rights that protect their work, and those rights can serve as an arbitration mechanism in a conflict between two parties. The Japanese, however, have a different perspective on the use and adaptation of others' ideas. They strongly believe that in their society rigid adherence to certain individual rights is a sure formula for instability and disorder. With 120 million people on a small land mass, there is not enough of anything—space, natural resources, or whatever—to go around; and arbitration usually involves compromising what may be construed as rightful claims, spreading the pain between two parties rather than deciding in favor of one party at the expense of the other. Similarly, intellectual property owners are expected to be reasonable about the return they obtain from their ideas instead of staking out their claims. During the 1960s and 1970s, Japanese industrial policy reinforced this perspective by discouraging passive income and rewarding people for physical productivity.

Other Asian countries are affected by these factors to some extent, but as we have seen, the Japanese have enjoyed a unique luxury in being able to pick and choose the foreign ideas they imported and adapted. The Japanese excel at taking foreign ideas, adapting them, and incorporating them into their own way of doing things. (Thus, Western words imported into Japanese are completely internalized; such a word is called *gairaigo:* for example, *nighter* means a baseball game played at night.) Unfortunately, the originator of the idea does not get much credit. Some recent painful experiences, such as the Hitachi "spy incident," in which a Hitachi employee was caught receiving sensitive information from IBM, and the Fujitsu/IBM arbitration regarding operating system software, are driving a slow change.

Some partnerships have gone through turmoil because of intellectual property. About ten years ago, Motorola licensed its 68000 microprocessor architecture to Hitachi. It is rumored that Hitachi took the vast majority of the 68000 microprocessor business in Japan. Not only did Motorola not license Hitachi on its next-generation product, but it entered into an extensive joint venture with

Toshiba. To replace the hole in its product line, Hitachi conceived its own series, called the H-series, and also aligned itself with the TRON project, a Japanese consortium. A few years later, Motorola sued Hitachi for infringement, and Hitachi has countersued Motorola, all in connection with the H-series product line.

Differing Views of Trust and Ethics

In chapter 2, I defined *trust* in the Japanese sense of the word as acting in line with Japanese norms of behavior, and noted that it was not directly related either to being able to lean on someone or to not being betrayed. The idea of competition and cooperation, which I have mentioned several times, also adds discomfort to Japanese-American partnerships. One often hears of a situation in which an American corporation finds that its Japanese partner is about to enter a partnership with a competitor of the American company. *Nikkei Business* reported that a partnership between Mitsubishi and TRW fell apart when Mitsubishi joined hands with Philco, a competitor of TRW.

Talking about ethics is difficult in general and almost impossible in an international context. But the concept of fairness comes up so often that it calls for some comment. American culture painfully strives for—if it cannot attain—fairness in the sense of equal treatment regardless of age, sex, color, or national origin. That is probably the only way to reach the noble goal of *e pluribus unum*. The cohesion of group behavior in Japan, however, tends to create factions even within organizations. The Liberal Democratic Party has many factions; so have large Japanese companies.

Many different groupings also cut across organizational lines. The cohesion of the group is maintained through a defensive orientation that requires a member to guarantee that any newcomer will subscribe to the group's norms of behavior. This phenomenon leads to people within the group being treated very differently than people outside of it. It certainly is not egalitarianism Western style. This difference manifests itself clearly when in partnerships between American and Japanese firms the Japanese side appears to be defensive about either certain classes of information or certain activities.

I learned about how groups work in this manner through a frustrating experience. A number of years ago, I was involved in proposing a joint venture to a reputable Japanese firm. A director of the Japanese firm asked us repeatedly to keep the discussion under wraps, and we asked him to reciprocate. He specifically requested that we not talk with anyone else in his organization until he thought the time was ripe. We were careful to keep even our internal communications restricted, and it was a well-kept secret—or so I thought. One day, over dinner, a person working for a distributor in the same business began to tell me about the supposedly secret arrangements, explaining their advantages and disadvantages. He had heard about the deal from someone in the Japanese firm we were negotiating with, but he would not pinpoint the source. In the Japanese culture, it is expected that people will share even extremely confidential information with others within the tight coupling. Furthermore, the rules are that such information can be used to the advantage of the recipient as long as the source of the information is not divulged. That is fairness, Japanese style.

Antitrust Practices

In the United States, five types of antitrust violations are familiar to most businesspeople: collusion, price fixing, market/customer segmentation, tying, and restricting vertical relationships such as those with distributors from free competition. In Japan, the antitrust laws are written to be practically the same in interpretation; any Japanese businessperson would say, if asked, that all these things are illegal.

The Japanese, however, strongly believe that in an island country as small as Japan, completely laissez-faire competition would lead to disastrous turmoil in the marketplace. They have therefore striven to create a system in which the various players in the marketplace—suppliers, distributors, and customers—operate in an orderly manner, averaging and sharing the wealth. Such a system necessitates loose enforcement of antitrust laws.

Those who have operated on both sides of the Pacific recognize this gap in sensitivity toward antitrust issues. Matsushita was recently questioned in the United States about pressure allegedly put on a distribution channel for consumer appliances not to discount below a certain level; apparently, a financial settlement was reached. In Japan, NEC was recently charged with trying to control the resale pricing of personal computers, and the company was given a "written warning." Such a warning is a dishonor in Japan but, clearly, represents far looser enforcement than would be found in the United States, where executives can end up in jail for that type of activity.

The foreign firm that engages actively in marketing partnerships has to be flexible in this regard. Probably every foreign businessperson in Japan has been approached by a Japanese firm regarding subtle market segmentation, pricing control, and the like. Currently, however, the extraterritoriality of U.S. antitrust laws makes it impossible for American firms to participate in such arrangements to the extent that the Japanese do. Thus, the American government has pressured the Japanese government to strengthen enforcement of Japanese antitrust laws under the structural impediments initiative.

Differences in Business Philosophy

The classic goals of American and Japanese corporations—profit versus market share—frequently clash in a partnership. Such differences in overall orientation affect many tactical decisions; and when these gaps surface, firms often reach an impasse. Decisions about jointly entering and exiting businesses are also difficult.

One specific problem in partnerships is that one of the partners does not have as much flexibility as the other in terms of the scope of the business they will engage in. Japanese journals have reported two examples of such differences. Duskin, which bought the Japanese marketing for Mister Donut, tried to partner with Long John Silver, the seafood chain, to penetrate the Japanese market. Test marketing found that the taste needed a little modification and that rice should be added to the menu. The U.S. firm decided that that was too much modification, and the endeavor never took off. During the 1970s, Mitsubishi partnered with Avis Rent-a-Car, but the arrangement did not work because Avis wanted to provide rental car service at airports, as in the United States, whereas Mitsubishi wanted to get into the lease business.

Differing Notions of a Relationship

In the United States, partnering is often equated with deal making. Getting a good deal is what an executive must demonstrate, given the shortness of the typical tenure in any one position. A successful long-term relationship is not rewarded as highly.

By contrast, Asians view partnering relationships in more of an emotional or, to put it more extremely, superstitious way. The two concepts that come to mind are *en* and *jyo*. There are no direct translations for these words in English; the concepts are uniquely oriental. *En* refers to a bond between two people or parties that is the result of luck. When people meet naturally and repeatedly under favorable conditions, they say there is *en* between them. For another set of people, Murphy's Law strikes: whenever they meet, something goes wrong. They say there is no *en* between them. Though based on superstition, the feeling that they have good *en* can create momentum in a relationship between two parties.

Jyo is another difficult concept to explain. It is akin to warmth, a feeling passed from one person to another that makes them feel closer to each other. The concept is related to empathy: "I think I know how you feel" is an English expression of *jyo*.

These two concepts form the core of what is called the "wet" oriental relationship. Although all business relationships the world over have a personal component, in Japan the influence of this "wetness" is very significant. When a relationship has both *en* and *jyo,* the parties try to stick with each other through thick and thin.

The American relationship is "dry" by comparison. Everything is businesslike, and return and profit are the overwhelming motivations at every turn. A significant change in the environment or a stress in the relationship may well sever or change a relationship. Such relationship reversals are seen all the time in the United States and even accepted as a way of life. They are less common in Japan.

This difference in orientation manifests itself in the frequent Japanese complaint that the Americans are cold. The American tendency to charge a partner for additional service, for example, is likely to be regarded in this way.

Differing Styles of Administration

In the United States, it is important to be in control of one's environment. It is even more important for a manager to be in control. The way to do this is systematic: in a joint venture, majority ownership is important; for other types of arm's-length partnerships, a binding contract covers all contingencies. That is how Americans work their "peace of mind" into a relationship arrangement.

In contractual agreements, businesspeople in both the United States and Japan understand that quantitative terms and conditions—such as costs, royalty fees, and delivery dates—must be set. When it comes to the "what if"s, however, the Japanese are not accustomed to spelling out every contingency in a contract. For example, no contract is signed between an author and a publisher in Japan. If something goes wrong, a discussion governed by accepted Japanese norms of behavior leads to a mutually agreeable solution.

The parties are little concerned about what provisions might stand up in court, because in Japan disputes are seldom settled in court. In contrast to American society, where lawsuits are frequent (another sign of a loosely coupled, confrontational society), the Japanese consider going to court to be the unfortunate final resort, because the result is usually destructive. First, all the entities whom the parties in the litigation deal with will treat these firms with skepticism, feeling that something must have been really wrong if they could not "keep it off the streets." Second, a clear-cut legal case makes it impossible to avoid pinpointing responsibility within the organizations, which goes contrary to the Japanese reluctance to assign praise or blame to individuals. The result is the truncation of one or more careers—a difficult situation for both employers and employees in a permanent employment scheme.

In many partnership negotiations in Japan, the Japanese have told me that it would be enough to put their wishes in the *gijiroku,* a set of minutes of a meeting that is not legally binding. They are saying that the Japanese behavior of not going back on one's word is sufficient. While this may seem unenforceable from an American standpoint, actually it is quite binding. Cultural commitments in Japan tend to be stronger than legal commitments; it is the intent, not the letter, of the agreement that must be upheld.

Nevertheless, when the American side puts down a laundry list of contingencies, the Japanese negotiator reviews it carefully, especially since it will have to be circulated for *ringi* ("consensus"). Moreover, if the contract is under the legal jurisdiction of the U.S. courts, it is only prudent for the Japanese to scrutinize it.

As to taking comfort in majority ownership of joint ventures, one look at a list of such entities formed between American and Japanese firms attests to the fact that majority ownership and business success are independent factors. There are U.S.-dominated joint ventures that have failed and U.S. minority equity positions that have succeeded and that provided the U.S. parent firm with all it wished.

Both American and Japanese firms make use of power and leverage in working their partnerships toward their own strategic objectives. The only difference is that the use of power and leverage is less overt in Japan than in the United States. According to the Japanese mode of "competition and cooperation," a firm with which one is negotiating could at the same time be a customer. An unsubtle leveraging tactic could backfire through a different channel, even long afterward, because of the long organizational memory that results from a low turnover.

Environmental Changes

Relationships can be structured to be as specific or as ambiguous as the partners agree. The American view is often that vague relationships are too noncommittal, and that neither side can hold the other to anything. The Japanese, on the other hand, talk about "umbrella agreements" or "gentlemen's agreements," which indicate nothing more than that the two companies will continue to have exploratory discussions on mutually beneficial topics.

In the majority of cases, partnership agreements are rather specific and assume a certain set of conditions— those that exist at the time the agreement is made. These conditions can change; as I pointed out earlier in the chapter, a manufacturer may be willing to subcontract in times of excess capacity, but when demand is strong, the subcontractor may discourage such arrangements. In the extreme case, a joint manufacturing venture conjured up during a boom economy could end by putting significant strain on one of the partners during a recession.

Resource Allocations and Interface Issues

Partnerships are supposed to be synergistic, particularly in terms of resource deployment. That idea can, however, lead to the illusion that one can get away with putting fewer resources into managing a partnership than are actually needed. As a result, partnerships sometimes suffer from undercommitment.

When one side commits significantly more resources than the other to the management of the partnership, the side committing more resources can become frustrated at the lack of support from the other side. One situation in which this phenomenon manifests itself is distribution relationships. A distributor can be content over the long term investing much less in the marketing of a supplier's product line than the supplier desires.

An important aspect of partnerships between Japanese and American firms is interfacing at different levels of the organization. It often becomes crucial to use different players to break an impasse. In the extreme case, a personal relationship between top executives of two firms may hold a partnership together for decades. In one situation where an American firm subcontracted the development of a certain product to a Japanese firm, the project went nowhere until a high-level executive from the U.S. firm called on his longtime friend in the Japanese firm. The project was completed expeditiously.

GUIDELINES FOR A SUCCESSFUL PARTNERSHIP

Partnering with the Japanese can go a long way toward enhancing a firm's competitiveness, either in Japan or worldwide, but the execution of such partnerships is, as we have seen, often hampered by cultural and motivational differences between the partners. Following are guidelines I have found useful in the partnerships with which I have been involved:

- *Balance global and local motives for partnering.* Partnering is merely one method of enhancing one's capabilities and improving investment efficiency. Any opportunities to be gained through partnering, however, should reflect a balance of the two types of agenda. This can be particularly important when an arrangement involves an exchange of technology (a global factor) for help in penetrating the Japanese market (a local factor).
- *Pick a compatible partner.* As we have seen, compatibility

in objectives is important. A match in cultural values makes interaction much easier; but if such a luxury is not possible, at least make sure that the prospective partner is willing to adjust and be flexible. There is disagreement on whether partners should have complementary functional strengths, but there are many examples of such contribution of strengths by both parties leading to synergy.

- *Negotiate hard for return, but only in the context of a positive-sum relationship for both parties; and structure the relationship properly.* Being a good negotiator is clearly a requirement for effective partnering. Part of that skill is being able to set up a win-win situation. One-shot, zero-sum outcomes, where one party reaps large returns at the expense of the other, cannot last long. It is also important to match both the timing of returns to the two parties and the costs to each of exiting the relationship. An arrangement in which one party gets a one-shot transfer of technology in return for long-term subcontracting will not motivate the subcontractor to sustain a high level of support for the project once the desired know-how has been gained. By the same token, if the unraveling of a relationship means the loss of a flow of technology to one party and a complete pullout from the country to the other party, the latter will be in a relatively poorer negotiating position in the long term. I always warn American high-technology firms to be careful about getting into exclusive distribution arrangements with a Japanese trading house, particularly if the foreign firm is going to depend totally on the trading firm's Japanese technical personnel. In the event that the Japanese firm decides to change suppliers a few years down the road, the U.S. firm would be in the position of no longer having a technical resource in Japan.

- *Commit the necessary resources to the execution of the partnership.* It is a general rule in business that the greatest strategies cannot succeed without good execution, and that even a second-rate strategy can succeed if executed brilliantly. The partnership cannot succeed without a full commitment of support. Though it is easy to think that the very reason for entering the partnership is to save resources, in fact many say that, in terms of management time, managing a partnership is just as demanding as managing a wholly owned subsidiary or a division. Whatever one saves by having fewer people and resources to manage is balanced by the overhead related to maintaining the relationship between two different firms.

- *Accept differences in culture.* It often does not pay in the short term to force one's partner to close the cultural gap. For example, it is better to accept that patience is key in Japanese business than to expect a Japanese partner to go through *ringi* (Japanese-style consensus decision making) unreasonably quickly.

- *Develop credibility on both sides.* It is good to partner with a firm one has some experience with; but when that is not possible, each partner should contribute something that results in a sizable accomplishment for the partnership. Nothing does more to gain trust and credibility than results and progress.

- *Follow established principles of management.* It is important to establish at the outset a set of ground rules that clearly define areas sensitive to the parties involved. Distinguish those tasks the U.S. firm must control and those the U.S.

firm does not mind the Japanese firm controlling. This process yields peace of mind to the Americans and *anshinkan* to the Japanese. Many firms do not bother to define these areas up front because it makes for tough negotiations, but it is well worth the additional effort. Once these guidelines are set, continuity and consistency in execution, particularly from the U.S. end, will help provide stability.

• *Keep contact at high levels.* It helps for high-level management from both sides to meet regularly to review performance and work issues. Such regular meetings are often used by the Japanese side to accelerate the resolution of a slow-moving *ringi* item. Executives at that level can also make a large difference in strategic direction and commitment of resources. Needless to say, preparation before such a meeting is crucial.

• *Anticipate problems.* Partnerships are living organisms. Environmental change may invalidate some of the terms and conditions agreed on at the formation of the arrangement. Dealing with such change before the pressure mounts reduces the trauma. A second reason for anticipating problems relates to the Japanese tendency not to give clear feedback. The Americans can learn more if they anticipate what might be going on below the surface, and take the initiative in asking about possible problems. The Japanese find it much easier to respond to specific questions than to a general query about problems.

• *Be flexible and willing to adjust.* This guideline needs no further explanation.

A partnership can be very effective, both in making a firm more competitive globally and in helping it become a semi-insider in a tightly coupled market such as Japan. Care must be taken, however, to position the partnership not as a shortcut to success but as an extension of one's capabilities and resources which requires a commitment to carry out the arrangement and maintain the relationship. With that commitment, the partnership can bridge the large cultural distance and effect cross-cultural penetration.

8

Survival of the Fittest

I BEGAN THIS BOOK by describing Japanese customer expectations and why Japanese culture drove them to such high levels. I then discussed how some American firms are coping with these expectations and with the Japanese business environment, and looked at marketing, human resource issues, and partnering. Considering the obstacles to success, one might well wonder why one should go through such trauma. That issue I addressed briefly in chapter 3, but let me now revisit it in a somewhat larger context— that is, my original premise that penetrating the Japanese market and maintaining global competitiveness are one and the same thing.

We are all witnessing the industrial version of the survival of the fittest. Globalization, a mandatory phase of industrial evolution, will test whether a given species—a certain American or Japanese industry—will survive. And in the context of globalization, survival is intimately tied to the ability of executives to venture beyond their rigid native cultural values and business practices. Having made the transition between the United States and Japan several times as a Korean citizen, I have been a relatively non-partisan witness to this dramatic process.

Moreover, the trend toward globalization has accelerated. When I first arrived in the United States, the average Asian thought of a trip to the United States as a once-in-a-lifetime experience. A ten-minute international telephone call was a major event one prepared for meticulously and conducted with a watch beside the telephone. Today I cross the Pacific at least once a quarter, often more frequently, and make international phone calls every day.

When I traveled between the United States and Japan in the 1970s, I used to bring gifts—American products for the Japanese and Japanese products for the Americans—that delighted the recipients. Now, not only do I have trouble finding things that cannot be bought in both countries, but the occasional gift I do find appropriate is often made in yet another country, sometimes Korea.

It is clear that in the industrial context national boundaries are quickly dissolving. Consumers can get products they want anywhere in the world. I currently live in Japan, but I bought an Epson printer (a Japanese product) in the United States and brought it back with me, saving 50 percent of what I would have paid in Japan. When Japanese subsidiaries of American firms sell products manufactured in Japan, which society gains—Japan or the United States? Mobility of industrial factors and information has made a world in which industry in geographic areas with relatively low competitiveness will either turn competitive or become extinct. Competition has intensified significantly and is becoming ever more unforgiving.

I learned engineering and management from two of the best schools in the United States. By the early 1980s, however, the Japanese had captured a significant worldwide share in a number of industries—automobiles, consumer electronics, and semiconductors, to name just a few; and I began to wonder why I had left a country with such industrial competitiveness in order to learn about excellence in engineering and management. On a recent trip to the East Coast, I was shocked at the industrial wasteland I saw from the window of an Amtrak Metroliner, especially in comparison with what one sees from the window of the bullet train in Japan. What has happened?

FACTORS HINDERING COMPETITION WITH THE JAPANESE

One reason for this rapid reversal is that basic American cultural values and business practices are faltering against industrial competition. Any organization, whether a country or a corporation, tends to grow significantly when its cultural values and business practices are consistent with and reinforce the economic output it is striving for. During the 1950s and 1960s, this consistency was manifest in America and there was sizable growth, but the situation has changed.

In February 1989, during the week of the funeral of the late Emperor Hirohito, all three major American networks anchored their evening news from Japan. They took the occasion of George Bush's homage to the late emperor as a chance to re-examine Japan. I happened to be in the United States then and watched many of the broadcasts. Much discussion concerned Japanese industry as a competitor to American industry, and much involved what the United States could do to "fight back."

The television programs focused mainly on what public policy options should be pursued in order to make Americans more competitive globally. The recommendations were not new. Becoming more team-oriented, with more emphasis on cooperation, is a respectable objective, but would require a major change in the American culture, particularly with respect to American individualism. I have in this book tried to show many of the ways in which individualism has made the United States a loosely coupled society, in contrast to Japan's tightly coupled society, and the ways in which it has shaped American business. The idea of an American version of MITI, for example, has been discussed and dismissed many times. Excessive emphasis on rights and confrontation has led to more unproductive disruptions in the United States than in Japan. Confrontational labor sometimes pushes firms into chapter-11 bankruptcy. The United States has a number of firms at whose economic scale the Japanese shudder. Many attempts have been made to take these firms apart. Industrial cooperation has been suspect, and antitrust barriers have resulted in fragmented efforts to compete with the Japanese. Finally, excessive individualism often leads to high turnover rates, with the result that in all but a handful of American firms retention of know-how is far less than one would find in many Japanese corporations.

The broadcasts also suggested changing the short-term orientation of the financial system, which places too much emphasis on quarterly results. The Japanese have unquestionably shown us the benefit of long-term thinking in many industrial settings.

Although most Americans would agree that the educational system needs an overhaul, little progress has been made in recent years. The American educational system creates excellence in a small percentage of its population; but aside from the top few, many people lack basic writing and arithmetic skills and have received poor training in attitude as well. Working hard and aggressively is starting to be looked on as abnormal behavior by some people—an effect apparent in the lax productivity and service of some U.S. firms.

Compared with Japan, the United States has been endowed with abundant resources. I still remember my amazement when I first came to the United States and saw that disposable products—paper plates, injection syringes, and so on—were widely used. I came to realize that there were good reasons for these products: disposable products are more sanitary, for example; and the labor required to clean reusable products is more expensive than the disposables themselves. But this mentality has led to tremendous waste in America on many fronts, including high overhead and cost structures, low productivity, and the sacrifice of young talents. Asian countries with fewer resources and higher population density place great emphasis on conservation, and a direct consequence is efficiency, an important aspect of industrial competitiveness.

I see a United States that is desperately trying to hold on, because none of its problems can be solved overnight. While many support the recent efforts to boost the yen, pry open foreign markets using threats of retaliation, and reinforce protection of intellectual property, I shudder at the possibility that these may represent the only short-term public-sector mechanisms for maintaining worldwide competitiveness. Meanwhile, American firms are struggling to compete on a worldwide scale. The problems underlying industrial competitiveness are deep-rooted and can be solved only in the long term, but I am reminded of a well-known quote by the British economist John Maynard Keynes: "In the long run we are all dead."

The good news is that there are actions American firms can take to enhance global competitiveness in a comparatively short period of time. Let me first, however, look at the problem of competing with the Japanese in one's own backyard.

COMPETING WITH THE JAPANESE
IN U.S. MARKETS

American industry has forfeited to the Japanese significant market-share positions in a number of major product areas. Much has been written about why this has happened, but in my view one of the reasons is simple: it takes less time for the Japanese to penetrate the U.S. distribution channels with a better quality, cost, delivery, and service product than for the American firm to modify its QCDS standards to meet the newly raised expectations of the American customer. As I showed earlier in the book, Japanese customers have been conditioned to be demanding of their suppliers. When suppliers who have lived up to those expectations penetrate the American market, American customers who were formerly tolerant of low levels of QCDS become more demanding. Suddenly American firms have to meet increased QCDS expectations.

In the early 1980s, for example, Hewlett Packard, a large

user of semiconductor devices, issued a report comparing the quality of Japanese dynamic memories with analogous American products. The significant gap embarrassed American semiconductor manufacturers, which have since tried hard to close the gap.

In the area of delivery, one American executive recently mentioned a phenomenon he had never before encountered in his long experience: his backlog was getting smaller and smaller. American customers are starting to expect very quick turnaround from order to delivery. One possible cause for this is that the just-in-time production system is being adopted by quite a few American firms, with the result that many supplier-customer partnerships are aiming toward reduction of order and manufacturing lead times.

With respect to production costs, when Japanese car manufacturers started taking market share away from their American competitors, one investigation revealed that Japanese automobile manufacturers had a $1,500 landed cost advantage: that is, an automobile produced in Japan and imported to the United States still cost $1,500 less than its American counterpart. Clearly, American customers welcomed that difference.

These examples are consistent with my own experience marketing products both in the United States and in Japan. Japanese customers are definitely more demanding, and American customers are becoming more so as a result of Japanese penetration of the American market. The idea that the Japanese are setting American expectations in some industries is no doubt repugnant to American businesspeople, but ignoring the phenomenon is tantamount to succumbing to the Japanese.

Why Play at Their Game?

Some may wonder why American firms should improve their operational capability. After all, perhaps American industry can never outdo the Japanese at their own game. Moreover, might not American industry lose its strengths in innovation by trying to improve operationally?

It is clear to me that there are two very different types of know-how: one that encourages revolutionary creativity, and one that encourages operational improvement. They both involve a variety of factors, including culture, motivation, the relative power of each function, and turnover. Just as many U.S. firms do not understand how their Japanese competitors can manufacture so efficiently, so the Japanese do not understand how Americans can do so many innovative things. The Japanese, who strive for orderliness and discipline, are baffled when Americans produce energetic ideas through a seemingly disorderly clash of polar thoughts. One of the most valuable things I gained from working in an American company was the understanding that managed chaos can lead to revolutionary breakthroughs. The excessive emphasis the Japanese place on industriousness hinders creativity. I once asked the late Dr. Robert Noyce, one of the developers of the integrated circuit, what creativity meant to him. He said that it involved finding a way around a problem. My perception is that when the Japanese confront a wall, they chisel it down little by little instead of looking for ways around it. One Japanese businessperson told me, "There is only one thing Japanese continuous process improvement cannot do— create something from nothing."

There is a danger in that observation, however. It is all too easy for American industry to take refuge in its strength in innovation, in the government's role in helping American trade, and in the feeling that the Japanese are unfair anyway—and to allow their operational capability to erode. American industry cannot survive as a design/development capability alone: that simply will not provide enough jobs. And those who believe that the United States can survive as a service economy should realize that little service economy will be left without the manufacturing sector.

Then there are those who argue that Americans should keep producing what they are good at—high-end products. Apart from the fact that producing high-end products automatically limits the number of units one can sell and therefore limits revenue, a number of risks are inherent in relying solely on such products. The first risk is that American firms will not be able to commercialize every new product generation they think up. Products fail for a variety of reasons not limited to their market viability: product development may have slipped and caused delays in product introduction, or the timing of the product announcement may be wrong. Venture capitalists in Silicon Valley are well aware of these risks. Unless the commercialization of the products has a high rate of success, a discontinuity in the market could allow lower-end competitors to creep up.

A related risk is that low-end products will replace high-end products. Two types of substitution occur at the low end: natural substitution and event-driven substitution. Natural substitution occurs when technology makes high-end products obsolete; quartz watches have reduced much of the demand for mechanical watches. Event-driven substitution occurs when some external condition forces a change in consumer buying patterns. The oil crisis played a key role in accelerating the substitution of low-end, fuel-efficient cars for gas guzzlers.

Thus, one must keep up with the technology and watch the market carefully. But fighting these lower-end products requires operational capability. The optimal strategy for American firms therefore has to be to innovate but to keep operational competitiveness at world-class levels so that, in case substitution occurs, they still can fight back. In keeping with the observation that innovation and operational competitiveness require different modes of operation, prudent firms are separating the organizations that produce high-end products from those that produce low-end products. One way to do this, as we have seen, is to place the high-end operation in the United States and the low-end operation in Japan.

My position, then, is that while American firms should continue to be innovative and differentiate their products/ services, they should also pay much more attention to operational competitiveness in the form of QCDS and not rest in the comfort of competitive barriers resulting from innovation. The QCDS level required to defend against market-share erosion may not have to match that of the Japanese competition but it cannot significantly lag behind either. The U.S. government should continue its efforts to encourage adjustment of the Japanese industrial structure, but this must be matched by the abovementioned effort by the private sector.

Problems in Learning from the Japanese

In addition to improving their operational capability, American firms must react when the Japanese strike. Every time there has been a threat from Japanese competition, however, American firms have taken an intolerably long time to respond. Those firms that are not semi-insiders in the Japanese market react first with neglect, then disbelief, and then foot shuffling.

Neglect often comes from a lack of information about Japanese competition. The biggest problem in this regard is that industry information and know-how generally flow from the United States to Japan; there is little flow the other way, for several reasons. To begin with, many Japanese businesspeople understand written English, but few American businesspeople understand written Japanese. Thus, in order to maintain industrial competitiveness, the Americans have a far greater need for translations and reporting from Japan than the Japanese need from the United States. Yet although two thousand titles are translated from English to Japanese every year, only about fifty are translated from Japanese to English. The four major networks in the United States provide only spotty coverage of Japan on their prime-time news broadcasts and maintain only small staffs in Tokyo; but NHK, the Japanese Broadcasting Company, maintains dozens of full-time correspondents in the United States. Nor can good market research on Japan be easily purchased. Because of the tightly coupled nature of Japanese society, it is difficult to find a penetrating and accurate piece of market research from a third-party firm. The American market research firm, by contrast, can tap recently resigned personnel for intelligence, for example.

Being able to read technical and business articles in both Japanese and English, I often compare what I have read in Japan with what is available in the public domain in the United States. Although reporting of general news on Japan is improving significantly, in terms of industry-related information from Japan the United States is a wasteland with few translations of Japanese technical or trade journals.

In any case, public information would be hardly enough to affect one's competitiveness. A firm must resort to in-depth competitive analysis, which often takes the form of a survey trip to Japan by key executives and factory-related personnel. I myself have hosted such visits by several hundred Americans to Japanese manufacturing plants and operations in a wide variety of industries, including electronics, food, and urgent-delivery services. I have also followed up to see what operational improvements have materialized as a result of these trips. My frank observation is that the yield from the trips is low.

The first part of the problem is that it takes an enormous amount of time before the observations of the visit translate into a general awareness that something at home should change. In the area of industrial learning in particular, American attitudes pose a significant barrier. American education often stresses positive motivation. Moreover, people learn at their own comfortable pace. Consultants compete to put on seminars that are entertaining; participants want ready-made answers, quick solutions, and personal involvement. That is often the way Americans learn.

The Japanese learn very differently. Students go through the so-called *juken jigoku* ("examination hell"), a grueling couple of years of preparation for a set of examinations that will determine their careers. No one honestly finds that fun. We have already encountered the concept of *shugyo,* where apprentices often get no positive feedback for years. The Japanese will learn even if the process is tough. They will learn at the pace set by the environment, and feedback comes in a vague form that one must aggressively explore in order to derive anything useful from it.

This difference in the learning process is apparent when Americans visit firms in Japan. I have held both preparatory meetings with Japanese firms, urging them to be open, and briefings with the American personnel prior to the visits. The trips have been organized to ensure that everything goes smoothly. But since Americans often want to learn in their own way, the information they get is limited to a superficial level.

A more serious problem has to do with perspective. Americans are frequently overconfident. By contrast, the Japanese tend to represent themselves as underachievers, even though in practice they outperform their competitors. I recently read that among thirteen-year-olds in six nations, U.S. students had the lowest scores in mathematics, while Koreans had the highest. Ironically, when asked if they were good at mathematics, 68 percent of the Americans said yes, but only 23 percent of the Koreans said they were. I detect a similar attitude with respect to Japanese competition; because of overconfidence and peer pressure to appear competent, Americans often do not look beyond initial representations by the Japanese.

When Americans visit Japanese plants, they seem to be there to evaluate rather than to learn. Instead of honestly accepting that the Japanese do some things better, looking for ideas for improving their own performance, and then defining action programs for improvement, they are more inclined to say, "The Japanese have their way of doing things, and we have ours. Maybe their way is good, but ours is good, too." When pressed about QCDS competitiveness, Americans often say that the problems have nothing to do with their methods but are organizational or in resourcing, for example.

Another mental block I often detect has to do with American views of competitiveness. Competition is relative—QCDS levels, for example, must be measured against those of other participants in the industry; but many Americans are starting to take a self-congratulatory attitude: "We're already doing our best. We're running as fast as we can." Unfortunately, those who take this attitude do not check to see how fast their competition is running.

Although I have criticized the learning attitudes displayed by Americans, it is plausible that the American style of learning may be better for development of revolutionary products, whereas the Japanese style may be better for operational improvement. The learning style, however, must be matched to the type of task. The Americans seem to use the wrong style for learning about the Japanese, and that is partly why the yield is so low.

Even when the appropriate learning style has yielded useful information, Americans take a long time to implement what they have learned. One Japanese businessperson told me that his firm is not as strict as it used to be about letting Americans into its plants; it is more sensitive about letting Koreans see its operations. Even though all the questions asked by American guests—including American competitors—are answered, little seems to change in the American operations back home. The Koreans, on the other hand, internalize their observations more quickly, and come back to haunt the Japanese.

Except for trivial applications, the ideas that an American plant manager or supervisor carries away from visiting a Japanese firm cannot be transplanted into the American corporation without major persuasion. Becoming operationally competitive implies making a significant change in the way things are done. It may mean, for example, that design engineers must share their elite role with manufacturing personnel. It also may mean a short-term sacrifice in profitability, which requires financial justification. Pricing aggressively to accelerate the scale and learning effects comes under margin scrutiny, and participating in a low-end product segment to counter a Japanese attack often encounters significant resistance from financial resources. David Halberstam, in *The Reckoning* (1986), eloquently describes the reaction of the Ford Motor Company when in the late 1970s the board considered a recommendation to develop a subcompact car. Finance advisors said Wall Street would not back such a project, and that was the end of it. These are uncomfortable adjustments that managers tend to leave for their successors to tackle.

In those cases where a proposal involving a gut-wrenching change is approved, executing the change is extremely challenging. Visiting a plant can give only a static picture of a competitor's operations or status. Just as one cannot modify a piece of software written by someone else to fit one's situation without understanding why it is structured as it is, one cannot adapt a process observed without understanding the dynamics that went into its development.

This, in a sense, is what the term "continuous process improvement" means. I am reminded of a trip I took with a group of Westerners to Mount Fuji, the highest mountain in Japan. Toward the top of the mountain, where the climb becomes quite steep, we took a series of fairly brisk climbs, each followed by a rest to recuperate. Meanwhile a Japanese party was moving steadily, step by step, without stopping. They reached the top much sooner than we did—the old story of the tortoise and the hare.

A Japanese business colleague once stated, "In Japan, if one stops running for one year [in terms of operational improvement], it takes three years to catch up." I realized the full implications of what he said during discussions with an American manager, who showed me a plan that he said would close the cost gap with the Japanese in five years. Five years later, he had met his cost goals, but his salespeople were still losing to the Japanese competition. He had met the Japanese cost position as it was at the start of the five-year period, but during that period the Japanese had obviously improved their position in cost effectiveness.

Small, incremental improvements can be undertaken even while larger changes are in the making. A group of American plant personnel visiting a Japanese plant observed that the Japanese workers were wearing masks and special footwear for dust control—standard practice in Japanese factories that produce medium- to high-precision products. The Americans commented that this would be easy to implement and would contribute to quality improvement. A few months later, they still had not carried out the idea. The reason, I was told, was that they were planning to incorporate the issue of dust-control gear into discussions about a major change in factory attire. After nine months, they made the change—but the benefits of the small improvement could have paid for the investment several times over if it had been implemented without delay.

Being able to sustain incremental improvements over a long period requires long organizational memories. Individuals and groups have to remember why certain actions were taken, what worked and what did not work, and how to adapt past experience to the present situation. The tight coupling of the Japanese firm and the low turnover make for a definite advantage here. Conversely, the high turnover characteristic of many American firms often leads to reinventing the wheel and repeating past mistakes.

For all these reasons, I have seen few cases of a successful static transplant from Japan to the United States. It simply does not work. Ironically, product know-how can be transferred in a manner closer to a "static transplant." When the Japanese receive technology from an American firm, it usually takes them much less time to internalize such know-how than it does for the American firm to statically internalize manufacturing know-how. Thus, to break this asymmetry, American firms must become more dynamic in their learning patterns—as I seek to explain in the next section.

Improving Performance through Semi-Insidership in Japan

Three types of American-based organizations are effective at learning operational know-how from the Japanese. The first category consists of those firms that actively participate in the Japanese market. These are firms like Fuji Xerox and Texas Instruments, which let needs of the Japanese customer drive their operational improvement. The key to their success here is that they often bring back to the United States both operational know-how and low-end products developed for the Japanese market. The second category includes those firms that are setting up joint-venture plants in the United States with the Japanese. If the American firm is not parochial and is open to new methodologies—a big *if*—the American side can accumulate a great deal of dynamic know-how from the actual experience of starting up and running the plant with the Japanese. The NUMMI joint venture between General Motors and Toyota is a good example of this type of effort, although it is not clear that other plants in General Motors are benefiting from the know-how. The third category is made up of American plants of Japanese firms. The turnaround after Panasonic (a Matsushita affiliate) acquired a plant from Motorola is well known. Sony's San Diego plant is functioning as a major supply source for the firm's American demand. And Honda's factory in Ohio is so successful that Honda has begun shipping cars made in the United States back to the Japanese market.

For American firms, this last category of success stories is not quite relevant. One reason that these Japanese plants in the United States are successful, however, is that personnel from Japanese manufacturing plants have taken what has already worked productively in Japan and modified it for their operations in the United States. In other words, they are not static transplants.

Manufacturing partnerships, the second category, can quite effectively help American firms become competitive. Start-up is relatively easy because of the partner's experience. There is one limiting factor, however. As we saw in the last chapter, partnerships are good only as long as the relationship lasts. They require commitment to execution, communication, and continuous negotiation.

That takes me back to the first category. Although using a manufacturing partnership is a good strategy for improvement, one of the few effective ways to keep operational know-how competitive over time is to participate in the Japanese market neck-and-neck with Japanese competition and strive to do three things: provide to Japanese customers low-end products that might become a factor in the American market; develop and introduce such products on time; and gain customer satisfaction through QCDS—quality, cost, delivery, and service. This means having at least semi-insider status in the Japanese market.

Look, for example, at Xerox Corporation. As the company that invented Xerox copiers, it sustained a major position in the copier business until the Japanese entered with low-end models. Xerox's share in the U.S. market was significantly eroded until Xerox's Japanese entity, Fuji Xerox, started supplying low-speed plain-paper copiers to Xerox for the U.S. market. Xerox's share in the U.S. market rebounded. Of course, it would have been better for Xerox if such a strategy had been pursued even before the dip in market share took place.

A SOLUTION TO THE TIGHT- VERSUS LOOSE-COUPLING PROBLEM

When I transact business in Japan and the United States, I am often reminded of the expression "divide and conquer." By using this classic military strategy, the tightly coupled Japanese business environment has wielded a considerable advantage over its loosely coupled American counterpart.

Japanese business has divided and conquered American business in many ways. The loose coupling between American manufacturers and their distributors and retailers has allowed Japanese firms to penetrate U.S. distribution channels. The loose coupling between American firms and their employees has often led to the loss of desirable people to the U.S. operations of Japanese firms. That, in turn, results in loosely held information as well. The financially oriented management of many U.S. firms has led to the sale of entire organizations and capabilities to the Japanese trying to penetrate the U.S. market. Moreover, the Japanese have used collaborative alliances to catch up with the know-how of excellent American firms in strategically important technologies. These tactics cannot easily be applied by American businesses trying to penetrate the Japanese market.

One solution to this asymmetry is for American industry to become more tightly coupled, and this is happening. There is movement to relax antitrust laws in order to allow greater collaboration between competitors. Sematech, for example, represents an American collaborative effort to regain competitiveness in the dynamic memory semiconductor business. Only time will tell whether these efforts will work out, but certainly the cooperation is there. American manufacturers also have been using their supplier power to discourage key distributors in their industry from carrying competitive Japanese products.

One could go further in this direction by becoming protectionist. The problem with this, of course, is that the United States has become so dependent on Japan as a source of end products, components, and manufacturing equipment that in many cases, without a non-Japanese alternate supply source, strong retaliation would hurt the United States. If the United States really played this kind of "hardball," its firms would have to develop alternatives to Japan for supply and financing, or prepare themselves for significant pain.

The other solution, which is often neglected, is to find and act on imperfections in the tight coupling of Japanese industry. Many people are inclined to think of Japanese industry as a monolith—"Japan, Inc."—but although this view may be useful at the public-policy level, in the case of private industry it simply discourages Americans from doing business in Japan. It may seem to Americans as though the Japanese act with a single mind, but from a business standpoint that is simply not the case.

The monolith premise ignores two fundamental facts. First, different Japanese firms and individuals do have different economic agendas that transcend culture and emotion. Second, Japan is changing, however slowly, and different firms and different people are at different stages of transition. An individual American firm doing business in Japan does not need to create believers out of the majority of the Japanese people in order to succeed. Such a firm can go a long way in Japan with one good partner, one out of ten customers, and one out of perhaps thirty distributors in the industry. The successful *gaishi*s mentioned in this book are not out to win a popularity contest and are far from receiving majority endorsement of their operations, but they have reasonable to excellent share and profit positions. Most of the Japanese competitors of IBM Japan would say that IBM Japan acts like a foreign company; yet a reasonable portion of the Japanese computer-user base says that IBM Japan provides Japanese-like service. That is enough to win.

This isn't to say that there aren't often practical ceilings to American market penetration in Japan no matter how good a firm is. The *Japan Economic Journal*'s survey of market share does not indicate many generic-product categories where a foreign firm is one of the top three in market-share position. Many *gaishi* executives talk about a market structure where they sense a ceiling to market penetration. One could argue, as the Japanese do, that any sense of such a ceiling is the result of aggressive "catch-up" by Japanese competition.

If there is a ceiling, the U.S. and Japanese governments should continue to work on the structural impediment issues so that such ceilings are raised and eventually removed. Meanwhile, it should be the responsibility of U.S. industry to maximize their market penetration at least to the level of that ceiling. Many American firms in Japan have market-share positions in the low single-digit percentages. They can certainly do better than that through improvement in QCDS ability, for example. Henry Kissinger recently made a comment that illustrates this point well: "Japan imports about eighty thousand cars per year. That's probably not enough. But, out of that eighty thousand, only two thousand five hundred were from the U.S.

That's not discrimination. That says something about what the Japanese public thinks about American cars." It is interesting to add that most of the rest of the eighty thousand come from German manufacturers like BMW, who have invested significantly in distribution channels and in quick-turns spare-parts warehouses, in Japan. Thus, the cumulative effect of each U.S. firm's maximizing penetration levels is sure to have a significant positive effect on the U.S. trade balance with Japan.

Looking further at the successful *gaishi*s in Japan, one spots a consistent theme: all have effectively segmented the Japanese. They have divided and conquered. The examples are many:

- In the area of hiring, we saw how Nihon DEC targeted maverick but effective Japanese new college graduates and lateral hire candidates.
- In marketing, BMW Japan has effectively targeted Japanese yuppies and has even induced Nissan Motors to introduce the Cima as a catch-up strategy. Fujita Den of McDonald's Japan has successfully capitalized on the trend toward eating out and now declares that his ambition is to get rid of the Japanese kitchen. As can be seen in Akihabara, the electronics retail section of Tokyo, the vast majority of personal computers manufactured by NEC, the leader in the product category, use American-made Intel microprocessors as the main CPU (central processing unit), despite the determination of NEC's semiconductor division to promote its own V-series microprocessor. A fact not often mentioned is that because most *gaishi*s are not closely tied to a particular *keiretsu* ("industrial group"), their neutrality allows them

to deal with more customers, particularly in the industrial area, than a Japanese *keiretsu* firm might be able to do.

- Many successful partnerships have been forged when diversification needs have been satisfied on both sides. As we have seen, Fuji Film wanted to diversify into xerography, and Xerox wanted to have a market position in Japan. The product-for-geographic diversification trade has produced other long-lasting relationships, such as Yamatake Honeywell in building controls and Mitsubishi Caterpillar in industrial vehicles. When one is looking for partnering motives, it is important to consider the various motives of firms that are already members of what may look like a Japanese consortium. For example, in the area of personal computers, although NEC is a member of the TRON endeavor (a project aimed at creating a Japanese-driven standard in operating systems and microprocessor architecture), it is not actively engaged in BTRON (the business-oriented TRON operating system) because of its dominant position in the Japanese personal computer market. NEC would have little incentive to be actively involved.

Thus, those who have been successful in Japan have not viewed Japanese industry as monolithic. The U.S. government can help private industry segment the Japanese not by praising Americans who have helped sell American products in the Japanese market, as it recently did, but by praising Japanese individuals and firms that have helped American products penetrate the Japanese market.

From the Japanese standpoint, anything divisive sounds evil. In fact, however, becoming a multifaceted society and economy is the only way that Japan can become a member of the international community. Greater differentiation and segmentation, even as a result of working with foreign entities, will contribute to what the Japanese themselves call *tayooka* ("coping with diversified needs"), a healthy trend for the Japanese.

To employ this "divide and conquer" strategy, the American firm must become a semi-insider in Japan. It is virtually impossible to recognize subtle segmentations in Japanese society and industry from across the Pacific. In accordance with Julius Caesar's *Veni, vidi, vici,* one must first come in order to see and conquer. I have often thought that American firms that have or will have Japanese competitors should send their CEOs to Japan for three to six months. It takes "the best and the brightest" in a corporation to perceive such segmentations and at least that long for such people to get a feel for how Japanese business practices affect the foreign firm. It also takes at least that long for American CEOs to understand their own foreign subsidiaries in Japan.

Despite the problems associated with long-term transfers, many firms have prepared contingency plans for CEO absence, and some even provide their CEOs with sabbaticals and leaves of absence. The potential benefits of an extended stay in Japan by an American CEO are many. The company and the CEO attract considerable attention from the press. It becomes harder for Japanese customers, partners, and others to criticize the firm for not being committed to the Japanese marketplace. The presence of a high-level officer provides entrée to all sorts of people whom the Japanese subsidiary by itself might not be able to engage. Moreover, it exerts positive pressure on the Japanese subsidiary to put its best foot forward. At the end of the period together, the CEO and the Japanese subsidiary should co-own the problem of Japanese market penetration, along with a set of cultural values that work across the Pacific. Last but not least, it greatly helps the firm's worldwide competitiveness. My view is that this is a far more effective way of tackling the Japanese market and competition than trying to run a Japanese subsidiary from across the Pacific by remote control. Any takers?

Of course, those who are sure that the Japanese will never become a major force in their industry can rest in comfort. But these things are never that easy to predict. It has often been said that the Japanese will never attain a major position in the American personal computer market. Even in the early 1980s, the logic was that the Japanese would never be creative enough to develop competitive software, a key aspect of marketing personal computers. Also, many claimed that since the human interface aspects of personal computing were culturally influenced, the Japanese would be at a disadvantage.

Never say never. Today it is not an exaggeration to say that the personal computer industry has all the characteristics necessary to make it the next area of trade contention. Without passing judgment on either the Americans or the Japanese, I should like to discuss the current situation.

As mentioned in chapter 1, Japanese manufacturers have developed their own personal computer standards which are completely distinct from any American-driven standard. Whether the Japanese legitimately needed to create a separate standard is often debated, but a recent effort to extend an American standard promulgated by IBM attests to the fact that Japanese language capability can be incorporated using such an American standard. The Japanese standards are only selectively open in contrast to the past IBM standards; hence, third-party software and hardware vendors are not completely free to develop products around the standards. The dominance of Japanese standards in the Japanese marketplace has made the marketing of American personal computer products in Japan an uphill battle: even major participants such as Compaq have no position in Japan. From the point of view of the multinational corporate user, such Japan-only standards prohibit one from owning a machine that can simultaneously play a wide variety of American and Japanese software.

Meanwhile, in the U.S. market, much has changed since the early 1980s. Two things have happened to accelerate Japanese penetration. The first is the wide adoption of the IBM personal computer standard, which gave Japanese competitors a target on which they can improve, and a foundation that allows any creative piece of software written on that standard to play on the Japanese machine as well. Second, the advent of a new category of computers at the low end—portable computers, notably the notebook computer—has changed the basis of competition at the low end in favor of the Japanese.

The portable computer is the epitome of the type of product at which the Japanese excel. To begin with, the Japanese possess all the component technologies—the flat panel displays, the circuit board substrate technology, the battery technology, the peripheral and power supply technology, to name a few. Also, from a manufacturing standpoint, as miniaturization of the product drives reduction in circuit board area, implying the attachment of semiconductor chips directly onto the circuit board unpackaged, precision in manufacturing becomes even more important.

If only one chip in more than a hundred does not work, one might have to throw away the whole board. As the semiconductor industry showed, yield-oriented manufacturing (where rework is either impossible or very costly) is a Japanese forte.

The end result is that today the top participants in the portable computer arena are either Japanese manufacturers or Western manufacturers that are subcontracting product with extensive Asian content. It is another VCR industry in that no American manufacturer can put significant content on American soil. There is much debate about what portion of the overall personal computer market this portable arena will capture, but this is reminiscent of the debate about Japanese low-end automobiles.

Not only does this repeat the typical scenario that occurred in industry after industry—Americans having a marginal position in the Japanese market, and the Japanese inching up in the American market from the low end—it also brings to light the American computer industry's dependency on Japanese suppliers. As a person who has tried hard to convince the Japanese to "buy" rather than "make" as the Americans do, I sometimes wonder whether this "buy what you can" philosophy is what discouraged American manufacturers from investing in this technology. And the steadfast refusal by the Japanese to change from *jimaeshugi* ("self-sufficiency") has led many Japanese manufacturers to state proudly, "We can make portable computers with internal technology." There does seem to be a tradeoff between free market and competitiveness.

Compaq, a firm known at its inception for transportable computers, introduced a notebook computer in the U.S. market in 1989. The product has significant content from

Citizen, a Japanese firm. Actually, my claim would be that if American computer producers had been stalking the Japanese market, they would have realized that the forerunner of the Japanese thrust into notebook computers was something called the Japanese portable word processor. Many Americans have seen this product in Tokyo, but that is not enough. One must look at the various technologies that make that product possible—displays, printed circuit boards, and so on—all of which are similar to those in the portable computer. This probably would have made it possible for American manufacturers to react faster.

The only temporary barrier that might slow the current Japanese thrust up-market from portable computers is the 100-percent retaliatory duty that has been put on 16-bit personal computers and above imported from Japan. This went into effect as a countermeasure to the section 301 complaint filed by American semiconductor producers. But this will halt the Japanese only for a short period, until they have their American-based operations in full swing. Let us look at this process further.

Japanese firms have excelled in the world markets in the past largely through an export-oriented strategy. Perhaps at one time huge centralized factories in Japan, controlled by Japanese headquarters, spewed products out into world markets. To cope with trade friction and globalization, however, some Japanese firms are adopting a multiheadquarters strategy—for example, one in Japan, one in the United States, and one in Europe, each with its own operations. This strategy makes competition less subject to trade restrictions and more dependent on basic competitiveness.

In addition, more Japanese firms are building local factories in the United States. Toyota has started up a plant in Kentucky. NEC is expanding its semiconductor plant in Roseville, California. Moreover, they are expanding their product lines into the higher-price-point areas because of competition from the newly industrializing economies.

Some Westerners have doubted that the Japanese could make the cultural changes needed to function effectively in the global market as well as in higher product categories. Even in the Japanese market, however, future-oriented Japanese firms are moving away from some of their traditional business practices. Where they once stressed market share, a perspective made viable by their financial stability, they are now looking for profitable opportunities in coping with exchange rate volatility and the competition from newly industrialized nations.

Globalization in high-technology industries is forcing a number of changes in the direction of efficiency and quicker action. The Japanese are encountering a need to compromise with their pure human resource policies, as embodied in permanent employment and seniority-based pay. Many Japanese firms that have needed to diversify quickly have broken with the past and resorted to lateral hiring, thereby introducing heterogeneity into their organizations. They used to seek people who would conform to the existing organization; now they search for people who can contribute ideas. The seniority-oriented pay scheme reinforces teamwork but does not motivate individuals to excel; as a result, many firms are looking at performance-oriented compensation schemes. The conventional Japanese decision-making method is being challenged as well. The *ringi* ("consensus") system, once regarded as a good cross-check mechanism to foster participative execution, is beginning to be seen as cumbersome and time-consuming in today's fast-moving world. Although the Japanese still call their decision making *ringi,* they are changing their internal procedures to reduce the amount of necessary sign-off.

In order to cope with a global organization, some Japanese firms are replacing their old, introverted cultural values with a new, open set—as in the following sampling of Honda's corporate values:

- Respect for logic
- Efficiency
- Emphasis on localization (conforming to the local business environment)
- Creativity:
  Respect for ideas
  Challenge
  "The wise eagle shows its claws" (in place of the traditional saying, "The wise eagle hides its claws")
  Escape from ordinary linear thinking
  "No risk, no error, no progress"
  Demand should be created, not reacted to
  Carry one's own torch, do not follow others
- Quality
- Customer satisfaction
- No price increases, period
- *San-gen* (the three realities, from *gen* ["real"]): the front lines, real products, and equipment
- One owner, one task
- Equality and mixed-blood philosophy

Some of these values probably sound familiar to Americans. Indeed, the risk is that Americans reading the list may think that the Japanese are becoming like Americans, and thus that they themselves can just keep on doing what they are doing. Americans who respond this way should be warned of several things. First, the Japanese change only according to their own rules. They will not accommodate foreigners entering their own marketplace unless they feel pressure or the need to do so. Second, the cultural values listed here reflect QCDS and operational efficiency. The Japanese are not going to forget about manufacturing efficiency as they move toward opening their cultural values. Third, as a recent survey showed, Japanese want to avoid certain American attributes—namely, among others, strong shareholder orientation, hostile takeovers, short-term orientation, rigid job classification and division of labor, and cut-and-dried contractual dealings.

Not all Japanese firms are moving in this direction. It is beginning to be clear, however, that even in the Japanese market those electronics firms that can make quicker decisions are ending up with the higher market-share positions. Those who insist on traditional Japanese habits are floundering. But many powerful Japanese firms are aggressively investing in operational capability in the United States markets, and such cultural adjustments are almost certain to make them more effective.

WHO'S GOING TO GET THERE FIRST?

Whether the world likes it or not, the Japanese market will be pivotal in the age of globalization. Moreover, many researchers and visionaries are saying that the twenty-first century will be the age of the Orient. Japan is the leader in this thrust.

If the Japanese already dominate their own market and are strengthening their positions in the American and European markets but the Americans continue their conservatism in investing in the Japanese market, it is clear who will win in the long run. Investment in the Japanese market cannot be made on the basis of the next quarter's profitability or even profitability three years out. This contest is the industrial equivalent of the Darwinian survival of the fittest. American firms that take their Japan penetration strategy seriously will go on to compete internationally in the age of globalization. Those that are in industries with strong current and potential Japanese competition, but that rest in the comfort of their usual practices, will perish.

The participation of a substantial number of American firms in these endeavors is the only way for the United States to regain, sustain, and enhance its industrial competitiveness. Though the American government is doing much, waiting for it to level the playing field is not enough: it will take too long. In the meantime, private industry must hone its operational capability to world-class levels. Using the Japanese market to calibrate one's capabilities now is essential in industries that invite Japanese competition, and is becoming even more important as the centrally planned economies in the socialist bloc start to convert to a market economy. Competitiveness will be a key determinant in who is rewarded by these new opportunities. I truly hope that the United States will live up to this challenge. Only by meeting it can American industry remain healthy and Asian nations—including Japan—survive.

Bibliography

PREFACE AND INTRODUCTION

ABEGGLEN, JAMES. 1987. "Japan, from blue collar to banker." *Tokyo Business Today* (Aug.).

HEARN, LAFCADIO. 1906. *Japan: An interpretation*. New York: Macmillan.

KANG, T. W. 1989. *Is Korea the next Japan?* New York: Free Press.

LORSCH, JAY. 1987. "Baseball and besuboru: A metaphor for U.S.-Japan misunderstanding." *Speaking of Japan* (Nov.).

" 'Side letter' to '86 chip agreement creates furor." 1989. *Mainichi Daily* (28 Apr.).

CHAPTER 1. ARE JAPANESE CUSTOMERS FAIR?

FIELDS, GEORGE. 1987. "The Japanese consumer: Wise or stupid?" *Tokyo Business Today* (Nov.).

MATSUSHITA, KONOSUKE. 1989. "Shobai senjutsu 30 kajo" (Thirty guidelines for sales strategy). *Dempa Shinbun* (28 Apr.).

SUZUKI, K. 1982. "Kikubari no susume" (May I suggest *kikubari?*). Tokyo: Kodansha.

"Betas (VCRs) never die; they just fade away." 1988. *Tokyo Business Today* (Mar.).

CHAPTER 2. BREAKING INTO THE JAPANESE BUSINESS ENVIRONMENT

CLARK, GREGORY. 1987. "Tribal moralities." *Tokyo Business Today* (July).

FIELDS, GEORGE. 1987. "Comparative advertising in a Japanese perspective: ASI market research." *Tokyo Business Today* (July).

WEISZ, J.; ROTHBAUM, F.; AND BLACKBURN, T. 1984. "Standing out and standing in: The psychology of control in America and Japan." *American Psychologist* (Sept.).

"Listing of noncompact VCRs." 1989. *Dempa Shinbun* (25 Mar.).

"Litigation is the American way, but all nationalities welcome to play." 1988. *Japan Times* (Oct.).

"When Keidanren speaks, everyone listens." 1987. *Journal of American Chamber of Commerce in Japan* (July).

CHAPTER 3. WHERE THERE'S A WILL, THERE'S A WAY

ABEGGLEN, JAMES. 1987. "Quiet success/Critics more outspoken." *Tokyo Business Today* (Nov.).

ALDEN, R. 1987. "Who says you can't crack Japanese markets?" *Harvard Business Review* (Jan.–Feb.).

Booz, Allen, and Hamilton. 1987. *Direct foreign investment in Japan: The challenge for foreign firms.* New York: Booz, Allen, & Hamilton.

HIATT, FRED. 1989. "Frustrated and defeated, a U.S. businessman says farewell to Japan." *Washington Post* (24 June).

IWAMURA, T. 1988. "The real thing: An American success story in Japan [Coca Cola]." *Speaking of Japan,* Keizai Koho Center (Feb.).

McKinsey and Co., and U.S.-Japan Trade Study Group. 1983. *Japan: Obstacles and opportunities.* New York: Wiley.

OKETA, A. 1988. "Gaishikei kigyo in Japan" (Foreign affiliate firms in Japan, Parts I and II). Tokyo: Dobunkan.

SCHOFIELD, MICHAEL. 1987. "Just another market." *Speaking of Japan* (June).

U.S.-Japan Trade Study Group. 1986. *Progress report.* Tokyo: U.S.-Japan Trade Study Group.

YOSHITORI, K. 1989. "Nihon kyofusho jyokyo ga senketsu" (The first order of business is to eliminate Japanophobia). *Japan Economic Journal* (21 June).

"Americans, Japanese say U.S. seeks scapegoat." 1985. *San Jose Mercury* (13 Aug.).

"BMW Japan: On a comfortable ride to success." 1989. *Tokyo Business Journal* (Feb.).

SURVEY JAPAN. 1982. "Breaking the barriers." Tokyo: Survey Japan.

"DEC Japan aims for top 5 [computer manufacturers in Japan]." 1987. *Tokyo Business Today* (19 Dec.).

"Foreign companies gaining foothold." 1987. *Tokyo Business Today* (July).

"Fujita-Den—Nihon McDonald." 1988. *Nikkei Business* (7 Nov.).

"Gaishikei kigyo no tainichi makikaishi sakusen" (The comeback of foreign affiliate firms in the Japanese market). 1984. *Jitsugyo no Nihon* (3 Dec.).

"Gaishikei shippai no kenkyu" (A study of foreign affiliate failures in Japan). 1976. *Nikkei Business* (30 Aug.).

"Heisateki shakai Nihon no shinwa o yabutta gaishi" (Foreign affiliates who have broken the myth of the closed Japanese society). 1983. *Nikkei Business* (7 Feb.).

"How U.S. high tech executives view Japan." 1986. *Electronics Business* (15 Jan.).

"Seiko suru gaishi, shippai suru gaishi" (Foreign affiliates that succeed, foreign affiliates that fail). 1985. *Toyo Keizei* (4 May).

"Shinka no kenkyu—Nihon IBM." 1989. *Nikkei Business* (16 Jan.).

"TI Japan: A winning subsidiary." 1987. *Tokyo Business Today* (July).

"U.S. manufacturing investment in Japan." 1979. Brochure published by the American Chamber of Commerce in Japan.

"Verity says U.S. firms slow to move in Japan." 1988. *New York Times* (12 Sept.).

"Zainichi gaishi no doko—Tettai ka zanryu ka" (The future of foreign affiliate firms in Japan—Pullout or stagnation). 1986. *Nikkan Kogyo* (Sept.).

CHAPTER 4. RESPONSIBILITIES OF A MAKER

ABEGGLEN, JAMES; AND STALK, JR., GEORGE. 1985. *Kaisha, the Japanese corporation.* New York: Basic Books.

CHANDLER, ALFRED. 1973. *The multinational enterprise.* Boston: Harvard Business School.

CROSBY, PHILIP B. 1979. *Quality Is Free: The art of making quality free.* New York: McGraw-Hill.

DARLIN, DAMON. 1989. "Myths about Japanese consumers fade." *Asian Wall Street Journal* (17 Apr.).

DAVIDOW, WILLIAM. 1986. *High tech marketing.* New York: Free Press.

HALBERSTAM, DAVID. 1986. *The reckoning.* New York: Morrow.

HAYES, ROBERT. 1981. "Why Japanese factories work." *Harvard Business Review* (July–Aug.).

HAYES, ROBERT; AND WHEELWRIGHT, STEVEN. 1984. *Restoring our competitive edge: Competing through manufacturing.* New York: Wiley.

Ministry of International Trade and Industry (MITI). 1985. *Selling to Japan from A to Z.* Tokyo: Ministry of International Trade and Industry.

Mitsubishi Electric. 1985. *Selling to Mitsubishi Electric: A guide to successful procedures.* Tokyo: Mitsubishi Electric.

NIHON KIKAI KOGYO RENGOKAI. 1987. "Gaikokukei handotaino access ni kansuru chosa kenkyu" (Research on market access of foreign-affiliated semiconductor manufacturers in Japan). Tokyo: Technova.

SCHONBERGER, RICHARD J. 1987. *World class manufacturing.* New York: Free Press.

WHEELWRIGHT, STEVEN. 1981. "Japan—Where operations are really strategic." *Harvard Business Review* (July–Aug.).

"How Japan overcame the high-valued yen." 1989. *Electronics Business* (20 Mar.).

"Japan strategy—Amex: Shinraisei o wasurezuni" (American Express in Japan: Reminding oneself of trust). 1987. *Nikkei Business* (31 Aug.).

"They [P&G] didn't listen to anybody." 1986. *Forbes* (15 Dec.).

CHAPTER 5. PEOPLE: THE KEY TO INTERCULTURAL OPERATIONS

ABEGGLEN, JAMES. 1988. "Expat managers or not?" *Tokyo Business Today* (June).

ABEGGLEN, JAMES, AND STALK, JR., GEORGE. *Kaisha, the Japanese Corporation.* New York: Basic Books.

KARASAWA, Y. 1985. *Gaishikei kigyo no genkai (The limitations of foreign affiliates).* Tokyo: Yuhikaku.

MIYAMOTO, N. 1986. *Nihon IBM—Kigyo bunka senryaku (The corporate culture of IBM Japan).* Tokyo: TBS Britannica.

RASMUSSEN, KAREN. 1987. "Moving to foreign firms is new executive trend." *Herald Tribune* (26 June).

"Gaishikei kigyo no nihonka—Nihon IBM no baai" (The Japanization of foreign affiliates—The case of IBM Japan). 1988. *Nikkei Business* (7 Nov.).

"Japan in America—Living in the U.S.A.—Japanese companies are racing to develop U.S.-flavored subsidiaries." 1987. *Electronics Business* (1 Aug.).

"Kraft named to head unit of Matsushita." 1989. *Asian Wall Street Journal* (May).

" 'Negative image' stifles U.S. recruitment in Japan." 1987. *Electrical Engineering Times* (23 Mar.).

"Nihon DEC: Shinjin kenshu no shiage wa beikoku e shugaku ryoko" (DEC Japan sends new college graduates to U.S. headquarters as finishing touch to new hire training). 1989. *Nikkei Sangyo* (14 June).

"Shocking facts about culture shock." 1987. *Tokyo Journal* (May).

"Yumearu shigotoga hikitsukeru. Daigaku yonensei survey" (The attraction of a job with a bright future). 1989. *Nikkei Business* (17 July).

CHAPTER 6. THE GLOBALIZATION OF HUMAN RESOURCES

CHRISTOPHER, ROBERT. 1986. *Second to none.* Tokyo: Tuttle.

FUJISHIMA, T. 1987. *Cross culture no jidai (The age of cross culture).* Tokyo: In-tsushin sha.

IKAWA, T. 1987. *Kokusaika jidai no kaigai chuzaiin (Overseas assignees in the age of internationalization).* Tokyo: Yuhikaku.

KAJIWARA, Y. 1985. *Nihon denki no soshikikasseika senryaku (NEC's strategy for revitalizing its organization).* Tokyo: Hyogensha.

PARTRIDGE, KATE. 1987. "How to become Japanese: A guide for North Americans." *Kyoto Journal* (Fall).

"Gaikokujin koyo—junketsushugi dewa ikinokorenai" (Hiring foreigners—You cannot survive with a pure-blood type of organization). 1988. *Toyo Keizai* (12 Mar.).

"How to be a global manager." 1988. *Fortune* (14 Mar.).

"Ikase kokusaijin no chie" (Benefit from the wisdom of international people). 1989. *Nikkan Kogyo* (15 June).

"Japanese executives relish the American style." 1988. *Asian Wall Street Journal* (1 Aug.).

"Nihonjin mura o sutete koso kokusaijin: Gijutsusha no beikoku funin" (One can become an international person only by leaving behind ties to the Japanese "village": The experience of a

Japanese technologist stationed in the U.S.). 1989. *Nikkei Business* (13 Mar.).

"Sodate, kokusai businessman" (Grow, internationally minded businessman). 1987. *Nikkei Sangyo* (26 June).

CHAPTER 7. CROSS-CULTURAL PARTNERSHIPS

ABEGGLEN, JAMES; AND STALK, JR., GEORGE. 1985. *Kaisha, the Japanese corporation*. New York: Basic Books.

ABEGGLEN, JAMES. 1987. "Shakeout of joint ventures in Japan." *Tokyo Business Today* (July).

DOZ, Y.; HAMEL, G.; AND PRAHALAD, C. 1986. *Strategic partnerships: Success or surrender?* Insead: London Business School, University of Michigan.

Nomura Research Institute. 1985. "Kantaiheiyo teikei shinjidai" (The new age of pan-Pacific partnerships). *NRI Search* (June).

REICH, ROBERT. 1986. "Joint ventures with Japan give away our future." *Harvard Business Review* (Mar.–Apr.).

"Chiteki shoyuken de Japan bashing" (Bashing Japan on intellectual property rights). 1987. *Nikkei Business* (15 June).

"Foster likes artful, one-on-one Japanese negotiating style." 1986. *Oregonian* (27 Apr.).

CHAPTER 8. SURVIVAL OF THE FITTEST

BUTLER, M. 1989. "A pro manufacturing U.S." *Electronic Buyer's News* (17 Apr.).

DRUCKER, PETER, 1987. "Beyond the Japanese export boom." *Wall Street Journal* (6 Jan.).

Fuji Xerox. 1982. *The history of Fuji Xerox*. Tokyo: Fuji Xerox.

HALBERSTAM, DAVID. 1986. *The reckoning*. New York: Morrow.

KOTLER, PHILLIP. 1985. *The new competition*. Englewood Cliffs, N.J.: Prentice-Hall.

LEE, O. 1982. *Chijimi shikoh no nihonjin (The tendency of the Japanese to miniaturize).* Tokyo: Gakuseisha.

LEVITT, TED. 1983. "The globalization of markets." *Harvard Business Review* (May–June).

MIMURA, YOHEI. 1987. "Global management: Internationalization of Japanese business." *Frankly speaking,* Keizai Koho Center (Sept.).

OHMAE, KEN. 1988. "Global consumers versus provincial government." *Japan Times* (19 Dec.).

President's Commission on Industrial Competitiveness. 1985. *Global competition, the new reality: The report of the President's Commission on Industrial Competitiveness.* Washington, D.C.: U.S. Government Printing Office.

PRESTOWITZ, C. 1988. *Trading places: How we allowed Japan to take the lead.* New York: Basic Books.

"Bush to review import quotas for steel." 1989. *Asian Wall Street Journal* (15 June).

"Detroit's cars are really getting better." 1987. *Fortune* (2 Feb.).

"The final frontier: Japan assaults the last bastion: America's lead in innovation." 1988. *Asian Wall Street Journal* (14 Nov.).

"How Japan wins battles in the trade war." 1986. *San Jose Mercury* (21 Apr.).

"How to beat Japan at its own game." 1988. *New York Times* (31 July).

"How to beat the Japanese." 1987. *U.S. News and World Report* (24 Aug.).

"Japan little concerned by U.S. chip plan." 1989. *Asian Wall Street Journal* (23 June).

"Nichibei high tech senso: Nihon kisogijutsu demo jishin" (U.S.-Japan high tech wars: Japan gains confidence even in basic technology). 1989. *Japan Economic Journal* (July).

"Nichibeioo HDTV kaihatsu senso" (The HDTV development race between the Japanese, Americans, and Europeans). 1989. *Nikkan Kogyo* (24 Mar.).

"Nihonteki keiei o toinaosu shacho tachi" (Japanese presidents who are reconsidering traditional Japanese management practices). 1988. *Nikkei Business* (12 Sept.).

"NUMMI—The best of both worlds." 1985. *Management Review* (Dec.).

"Wagasha no summit keiei kaigi: Top-down shiko sakkaku" (Our firm's top management decision making: The illusion of top-down orientation). 1989. *Nikkei Sangyo* (July).

"What Motorola learns from Japan." 1989. *Fortune* (24 Apr.).

"Who are the copycats now?" 1989. *Economist* (20 May).

"Why DuPont had to do R&D in Japan." 1989. *Electronic Business* (6 Mar.).

"Will Japan really change?" 1986. *Business Week* (12 May).

GENERAL

ABEGGLEN, JAMES; AND STALK, JR., GEORGE. 1985. *Kaisha, the Japanese corporation*. New York: Basic Books.

CHRISTOPHER, ROBERT. 1986. *Second to none*. Tokyo: Tuttle.

FALLOWS, JAMES. 1989. "Containing Japan." *Atlantic Monthly* (May).

HALL, E.; AND HALL, M. 1987. *The hidden differences*. New York: Doubleday.

HOUT, THOMAS; PORTER, MIKE; AND RUDDEN, EILEEN. 1982. "How global companies win out." *Harvard Business Review* (Sept.–Oct.).

IACOCCA, LEE. 1989. "Give and take." *Speaking of Japan*. Tokyo: Keizai Koho Center.

IBM Japan. 1988. *Nihon IBM—50 nenshi (IBM Japan—A fifty-year history)*. Tokyo: IBM Japan.

INSEC. 1989. "INSEC shuyo handotai user no jittai to gaikoku kei handotai saiyo e no torikumi jyotai." (Survey on status of Japanese semiconductor purchasers and their efforts to use foreign-made semiconductors). INSEC (Mar.).

International Forum of High Tech Industry. 1986. *Technology development in the 1990s*. Tokyo: EIAJ, Ministry of International Trade and Industry.

Keizai Koho Center. 1988. *Japan, 1988: An international comparison*. Tokyo: Japanese government publication.

————. 1985. *Trading with Japan.* Tokyo: Japanese government publication.

KOJIMA, K. 1978. *Japanese direct foreign investment.* Tokyo: Tuttle.

Massachusetts Institute of Technology. Alfred Sloan School of Management. Industrial Liaison Program. 1982. *Effective business management: Lessons from Japan.* Cambridge: MIT Press.

Ministry of International Trade and Industry (MITI). 1985. *134 sha no yunyu kakudai keikaku ni tsuite (The import promotion plans for 134 Japanese firms).* Tokyo: Ministry of International Trade and Industry.

————. 1988. *Gaishikei kigyo no doko (Trends in foreign affiliate firms in Japan).* Tokyo: Ministry of International Trade and Industry.

Mitsubishi Group. 1988. *Mitsubishi Fact Book.* Tokyo: Mitsubishi Group.

MORITA, AKIO. 1987. *Made in Japan.* Tokyo: Asahi Shinbun.

NEGANDHI, A.; AND GALIGA, B. 1981. *The tables are turning: German and Japanese multinational companies in the United States.* Berlin: International Institute of Management.

OHMAE, KEN. 1986. *Nihon keizaini kirikomu (Cutting into the Japanese economy).* Tokyo: Kodansha.

————. 1987. *Nihon kigyo ikinokori senryaku (Survival strategies for Japanese firms).* Tokyo: President.

————. 1984. *Triad power.* New York: Free Press.

PASCALE, RICHARD; AND ATHOS, ANTHONY. 1981. *The art of Japanese management.* New York: Warner Books.

Prudential Bache. 1989. *Japanese industrial electronics.* New York: Prudential Bache (22 Mar.).

SAKAMOTO, K.; AND SHINOYA, S. 1987. *Gendai Nihon no kigyo group (The group structure of Japanese firms).* Tokyo: Toyo Keizai.

SAKUMA, K. 1983. *Nihonteki keiei no kokusai-ka (The internationalization of Japanese management).* Tokyo: Yuhikaku.

Semiconductor Industry Association. 1985. *The impact of Japanese market barriers in microelectronics.* Palo Alto, Calif.: Semiconductor Industry Association.

YAMAMURA, K. 1989. "Keiretsuka wa heisateki ka" (Do Japanese industrial groupings lead to closed markets?). *Nikkei Sangyo* (July).

YOSHIHARA, E.; HAYASHI, K.; AND YASUMURO, K. 1988. *Nihon kigyo no global keiei (The global management of Japanese firms).* Tokyo: Toyo Keizai Shimpo-sha.

"1989 national trade estimate report on foreign barriers." 1989. *USTR* (Apr.).

"The Americanization of Honda." 1988. *Business Week* (25 Apr.).

"Are U.S. workers lazy?" 1985. *Industry Week* (10 June).

JAPAN ECONOMIC JOURNAL. 1988. *Book of {market} share.* Tokyo: Japan Economic Journal.

"Daitenho kaisei: Ryutsugyokai mo sengoku jidaini" (Modifying the regulations governing establishment of large retail stores: Japanese distribution industry headed for samurai war era). 1989. *Nihon Kogyo Shinbun* (June).

"Evaluation of manufacturing investments: A comparison of U.S. and Japanese practices." 1986. *Financial management* (Spring).

"Hakai suru Nihonno kakaku" (The collapse of the Japanese price structure). 1988. *Nikkei Business* (7 Nov.).

"Harvard experts' panel warns Japan, U.S. headed for war over trade." 1986. *Japan Times* (29 Oct.).

"Japan rivals U.S. in electronic output." 1989. *Asian Wall Street Journal* (May).

"Japan says U.S. complaint unjustified." 1989. *Asian Wall Street Journal* (June).

"Keizai senryaku. Glocal kigyo e no chosen" (Corporate policy: The trade-off between localization and globalization). 1988. *Nikkei Business* (26 Sept.).

"Kewashii yunyu taikoku e no michi" (The rough road to becoming a major importer). 1989. *Japan Economic Journal* (June).

"Managers strive to slice time needed to develop products." 1988. *Wall Street Journal* (23 Feb.).

"Nihon IBM. Ohkina kogaisha, zenhoi senryakuni mokeru" (IBM Japan, a large subsidiary: Profits through encirclement of competition). 1989. *Nikkei Business* (16 Jan.).

"Nihon kigyono kenkyu kaihatsu" (The R&D capabilities of Japanese firms). 1986. *Nikkei Business* (15 Sept.).

"Nomura chuki keizai tembo" (Nomura medium-term economic outlook). 1989. *NRI* (Apr.).

"N.V. Phillips is resisting Japan's electronics juggernaut: Dutch multinational company applies carrot and stick approach." 1987. *Wall Street Journal* (2 Feb.).

"Shinka no kenkyu—Honda giken" (The story of corporate evolution—Honda Motors). 1987. *Nikkei Business* (21 Dec.).

"Shinka no kenkyu—Matsushita Denki Sangyo" (The story of corporate evolution—Matsushita Electric Industrial). 1988. *Nikkei Business* (18 Jan.).

"Study shows hiring bias by the Japanese." 1988. *Herald Tribune* (16 Sept.).

"Yushutsu no beikoku banare susumu" (Japanese diversifying their export markets away from U.S.). 1989. *Japan Economic Journal* (13 June).

Glossary

THE FOLLOWING IS A LIST of Japanese business terms used in this book, along with approximate English translations and page references.

a un no kokyu (tacit communication and feedback) p. 122

akachochin (low end bar where bottom line opinions are exchanged) p. 148

amakudari ("descent from heaven"—the practice of bureaucrats retiring into private sector firms) p. 33

anshinkan (peace of mind) pp. 2, 7, 17, 18, 19, 20, 23, 24, 56, 59, 66, 111, 132, 138, 164, 185, 188, 190, 217

atarimae (common sense) pp. 38, 121, 165

"batting" (channel conflict) p. 46

byodo (fairness and equality) p. 143

"catch-up" (popular expression for a strategy used by a follower to catch up to and surpass the leader) p. 66

"costodaun" (reduce the cost) p. 78

dango (collusion) p. 39

danryokuteki unei (flexible enforcement) p. 36

donburi kanjyo (all-in-one pricing) p. 11

"dry" relationship (a relationship based solely on an official business arrangement) p. 209

eetokotori (taking just the good parts) p. 197

en (superstitious luck in the relationship between two parties) p. 209

gaijin (foreigner) p. 117

gairaigo (imported Western expression) p. 204

gaisha (foreign car) p. ix

gaishi (foreign affiliated company in Japan) pp. x, 110, 117, 118, 121, 125, 126, 127, 129, 130, 132, 135, 136, 137, 139, 140, 141, 142, 143, 144, 145, 146, 147, 148, 149, 150, 151, 156, 159, 240, 241

hanashiai (discussion/negotiation) p. 38

happobijin (looking pretty to everyone) p. 156

hesomage (emotional damage that is often unstated) p. 146

hosho (guarantee) pp. 56, 119

ichi o yueba jyu o shiru (know ten from hearing one) p. 60

itamiwake (sharing of pain) pp. 38, 56, 89

jikoryu (doing things according to one's own style) p. 122

jimaeshugi (self-sufficiency policy) pp. 19, 20, 246

juken jigoku (examination hell) p. 231

jyo (natural empathy in a relationship) p. 209

kaisha (Japanese corporation) pp. 41, 117, 118, 128, 131, 132, 149, 198

kamaseru (allow participation of others and share in the fruit) pp. 10, 56, 89

kanban (store sign or "brand") p. 77

keiretsu (Japanese industrial grouping) pp. 241, 242

kikubari (extreme sensitivity to the tacit concerns and needs of others) p. 16

kokusaika (Japanese version of internationalization) p. 168

komawari ga kiku (responding to requests quickly without exercising the whole organizational bureaucracy of the supplier) p. 16

koseki (family registration system) p. 23

kyoso to kyocho (competition and cooperation) pp. 38, 40

madogiwazoku (organizational deadwood) p. 129

mikomi hatchuu (expectation orders, or order entry prior to receiving formal order from customer) pp. 105, 106 *"missu"* (Japanese imported expression for "miss" or mistake) p. 94

muda, mura, muri (adversarial factors in managing a factory: waste, irregularity, and abnormal coercion) p. 96

naitei (a decision that has been made but has not yet been announced) p. 135

otokuisan (long-time customer, often exclusive) p. 43

"plus alpha minus beta" (an often-used Japanese product "catch-up" strategy) p. 83

ringi (Japanese-style consensus process) p. 162

satori (tacit inference) p. 170

sei-kan-zai-gaku (interdependent stakeholders in Japanese industry—politicians, bureaucrats, industry, and academia) p. 32

shakaijin (responsible adult and member of society) p. 177

shidoh ("guidance," direction) pp. 35, 36, 37, 39, 46, 134, 191

shikitari ("the way things are done around here") p. 121

shi-noh-koh-sho (class structure that existed in shogunate days: warrior, farmer, craftsman, and merchant, in order of superiority) p. 4

shinjinrui (the younger generation, new breed) p. 176

shinrai ("trust") p. 37

shitauke (subcontractor) p. 172

shugyo (apprenticeship) pp. 60, 142, 231

sogo izon (mutual dependency) p. 21

tatemae to honne (the official and real story) pp. 124, 125

tayooka (diversification) p. 243

tokumei/shimei (the practice of specifying a vendor to be dealt with, without full competitive considerations each time there is demand) p. 43

"wet" relationship (relationship in which multiple motives are mixed and transactions are effected without looking at individual profit items) p. 210

yokonarabi ("herd instinct") p. 40

Index